BARNDOMINIUMS

MAXIMIZE DESIGN EFFICIENCY FOR OPEN-CONCEPT
LIVING: A STEP-BY-STEP GUIDE TO CRAFTING YOUR
SUSTAINABLE DREAM HOME AFFORDABLY, DESPITE
BUDGET CONCERNS AND TRANSFORM YOUR VISION
INTO REALITY!

M.R. BOSS

TABLE OF CONTENTS

INTRODUCTION

Some moments in life mark the beginning of an adventure so profound it changes the trajectory of our lives. For the Johnson family, that moment came when they stepped into their newly completed barndominium. It wasn't just the expansive open-concept living area or the seamless blend of rustic and modern design that captured their hearts; it was the realization of a dream that many thought impossible. This home, a once plain and unassuming barn, stood transformed into a breathtaking abode, symbolizing not just a revolution in living spaces but a testament to what can be achieved with vision, determination, and a little guidance.

If you're wondering, "What exactly is a barndominium?" You're not alone. Barndominiums originated as a practical solution for living and working in the same space. They have become a symbol of versatility and innovation in modern home design. They combine the enduring charm of a barn with the comfort and style of a condominium, offering endless customization opportunities to fit any lifestyle.

Step into my realm: the realm of M.R. Boss, a pillar of creativity and innovation in interior design, especially within the barndominium sphere. My journey in transforming spaces, regardless of budget constraints, has been a calling and a passion that breathes life into achieving one's dream home. This book is the culmination of a dedicated effort to master the art of creating stunning, affordable homes, proving that luxury and budget can go hand in hand. It's a reassurance that your dream home is within reach.

Barndominiums: Maximize Design Efficiency for Open-Concept Living is not just a book; it's your comprehensive guide from the seed of an idea to the joy of moving into your dream home. Whether you're navigating the initial planning stages, tackling the complexities of construction, or adding those final, personal touches, this book promises to be your unwavering companion through it all. It's a support system for your dream home journey.

This book's structure provides a clear pathway to achieving your barndominium through the maze of decision-making, budgeting, and construction; it demystifies bringing your dream barndominium to life. Through the lens of real-life success stories and the tackling of everyday challenges, I offer practical, actionable advice tailored to various financial circumstances. My journey, filled with hurdles and triumphs, weaves through these pages, serving as a source of inspiration and a testament to the power of perseverance.

As we embark on this journey together, I invite you to approach your barndominium project with an open heart and a mind brimming with possibilities. With this book, you're building a house, crafting a sanctuary, a space where memories unfold and dreams flourish. Let's turn that vision into your reality, no matter your budget. Welcome to the transformative world of barndominium living. Let's get started.

1

UNDERSTANDING BARNDOMINIUM LIVING

W ithin the fabric of American innovation, a unique architectural phenomenon has woven itself into the hearts and landscapes of those daring enough to dream differently. This phenomenon, known as the barndominium, has transcended its humble origins to become a hallmark of modern, practical living. Its rise from mere functional structures to beloved homes mirrors the evolving aspirations of individuals seeking shelter and sanctuaries that resonate with their deepest values and desires.

THE RISE OF BARNDOMINIUMS: A MODERN HOUSING REVOLUTION

Emergence and Popularity

In tracing the ascent of barndominiums, one must acknowledge their genesis in the rural expanses of America. Initially conceived as a pragmatic way to house livestock and their keepers under one roof, these structures exemplified efficiency. However, as the winds of change swept across the architectural and cultural landscapes, so did the perception of these humble constructions. Visionaries saw beyond their functional origins, envisioning spaces where vast, open interiors could be sculpted into bespoke habitats. This reimagining sparked a transformation, propelling barndominiums from their agricultural roots to the forefront of a modern housing revolution. Their growing popularity is a testament to this evolution, with an increasing number of individuals opting for these adaptable structures as their primary residences.

Cultural Shifts and Influence

The barndominium movement has been significantly sustained by broader cultural shifts toward sustainability and minimalism. In an era where the collective consciousness leans toward reducing carbon footprints and living more conscientiously, barndominiums emerge as beacons of eco-friendly living. Their adaptive reuse of existing structures curtails the demand for new construction materials and champions the ethos of sustainability. Furthermore, the minimalist movement, emphasizing decluttering and living with intention, finds a harmonious match in the barndominium's open, unobstructed spaces. These cultural currents have influenced the surge in barndominium living and reshaped the narrative around what it means to create a home in the twenty-first century.

Comparative Affordability

An undeniable allure of the barndominium is its comparative affordability, especially poignant in an age where homeownership seems increasingly out of reach for many. When juxtaposed with traditional housing, the cost advantage becomes starkly apparent. The repurposing of existing barns or the use of prefabricated kits in constructing barndominiums significantly reduces both material and labor expenses. This cost-efficiency does not suggest a compromise in quality or comfort; instead, it presents a viable, attractive alternative for first-time homeowners and those navigating the constraints of a tight budget. It's a paradigm shift, redefining the pathways to owning a home that is both aesthetically pleasing and financially accessible.

Diverse Applications

The versatility of barndominiums is one of their most compelling attributes. Far from being monolithic, these structures skillfully accommodate myriad uses, reflecting the multifaceted lives of their inhabitants. A barndominium can be a sanctuary of warmth and togetherness for families, with ample room for each member to carve out their oasis. For the artist or craftsman, it offers expansive workshops where creativity knows no bounds. Those yearning to retreat from the bustle of urban life find solace in barndominiums nestled in nature, serving as vacation homes that rejuvenate the spirit. Moreover, the entrepreneurial spirit finds a home in barndominiums, with spaces seamlessly blending living areas with commercial ventures. This adaptability broadens the appeal of barndominiums and underscores their potential to mold themselves to the contours of any lifestyle.

Reflecting on the ascent of barndominiums within the architectural landscape, one cannot help but marvel at their journey from functional barns to characteristic homes. This transformation is not merely about evolving a housing trend but speaks to a deeper cultural recalibration toward valuing sustainability, affordability, and versatility in our living spaces. As more individuals seek to align their habitats with their values, the barndominium stands as a testament to the possibilities that emerge when we dare to envision beyond the conventional.

DEBUNKING BARNDOMINIUM MYTHS: WHAT THEY ARE AND AREN'T

In innovative living spaces, barndominiums stand tall, yet not without a shroud of myths that often cloud their true essence. One prevailing misconception is these structures' supposed limitations in design and functionality. Critics argue that barndominiums, rooted in agricultural utility, need more sophistication and versatility than traditional homes. This notion, however, wilts under scrutiny. The truth lies in the architectural freedom these spaces afford; far from being constrained, barndominiums serve as a canvas for creativity. The expansive interiors, unburdened by load-bearing walls, invite homeowners to carve out living spaces that defy convention. From airy lofts that bathe in natural light to cozy nooks that offer sanctuary, the possibilities stretch as far as one's imagination can roam.

Moving beyond the confines of design, questions often arise regarding the structural integrity of barndominiums. Skeptics question whether these repurposed barns or newly erected structures can withstand the tests of time and nature. However, this doubt dissipates when one considers the engineering aptitude behind modern barndominiums. Constructed with materials that honor tradition and innovation, these homes match and, at times, surpass the durability of their conventional counterparts. Steel frames, revered for their strength, form the backbone of many barndominiums, ensuring a steadfastness against the elements that rival any residential edifice. Furthermore, the meticulous attention to insulation and ventilation within these structures fortifies them against the whims of weather and enhances their energy efficiency, a testament to their resilience.

The discourse around barndominiums often circles back to their customization potential, a facet sometimes underappreciated in casual observations. Detractors might insinuate a rigidity in the architectural expression of barndominiums, yet this could not be further from the truth. The architectural DNA of barndominiums is inherently malleable, empowering owners to tailor their spaces to the intricacies of their needs and aspirations. Whether envisioning a home that embraces the raw aesthetics of industrial design or one that radiates a warm rustic charm, the barndominium adapts. This adaptability extends beyond mere aesthetics; it encompasses the functionality of the living space. Rooms flow into one another, each serving multiple purposes yet blending into a cohesive whole. This fluidity in design maximizes the utility of each square foot and reflects the dynamic nature of contemporary lifestyles.

Amid the dialogue surrounding barndominiums, their eco-friendly potential is sometimes obscured by misconceptions. Critics might cast a shadow of doubt, questioning the sustainability of these structures compared to other home types—this skepticism withers in the light of facts. Barndominiums, by their very nature, are paragons of sustainable living. Repurposing existing barns into habitable spaces is a practice in resource conservation, breathing new life into structures that might otherwise succumb to neglect. For new constructions, the choice of materials often leans toward those that are renewable or have a minimal environmental footprint. The design of barndominiums, with their emphasis on natural lighting and efficient use of space, further underscores their commitment to eco-conscious living. Moreover, incorporating green technologies, from solar panels to geothermal heating systems, transforms these homes into strongholds of sustainability. Thus, barndominiums challenge the idea that they are less green than other home types and position themselves as forerunners in moving toward more sustainable living spaces.

In confronting the myths that swirl around barndominiums, it becomes clear that these structures are not mere trends but pivotal in home design's evolution. They break free from the conventional, offering a place to live and a space to thrive. The limitations ascribed to them in design, durability, customization, and sustainability dissipate under scrutiny, revealing a housing option as robust and flexible as it is conscientious. In the landscape of modern living, barndominiums are not outliers but harbingers of a future where the home reflects one's values, creativity, and aspiration for a better world.

THE APPEAL OF BARNDOMINIUMS: COMBINING AESTHETICS WITH FUNCTIONALITY

In architectural design, barndominiums are a testament to the harmonious marriage of aesthetic appeal and functional pragmatism. These structures, with their roots deeply embedded in the practicality of rural life, have evolved to embody a design philosophy that celebrates the fusion of rustic charm with the sleekness of modern living. This evolution is not merely a trend but a reflection of a deeper understanding of how spaces can adapt to the multifaceted demands of contemporary life. In this context, barndominiums emerge as a compelling choice for those seeking a home that is both a sanctuary and a statement.

The aesthetic flexibility of barndominiums is one of their most enticing attributes. These structures defy the conventional boundaries of residential design, offering a canvas awaiting individual creativity's imprint. The inherent architectural elements of barndominiums, such as exposed wooden beams and metal accents, serve as nods to their farming heritage while providing a rich textural backdrop for modern design interventions. This juxtaposition of the old and the new creates a unique, timeless, and contemporary aesthetic. Homeowners are thus empowered to weave their narratives into the fabric of their homes, crafting spaces that resonate with their identities and aspirations.

Beyond their visual appeal, barndominiums excel in space efficiency by adopting open-concept living areas. This design approach not only maximizes the utility of every square foot but also fosters a sense of connectivity within the home. The absence of unnecessary walls and divisions allows light to permeate freely, creating an airy and inviting ambiance. This openness facilitates family interaction and togetherness, transforming the home into a dynamic space where life's moments are shared and celebrated. Similarly, for those who entertain, the seamless flow between living, dining, and kitchen areas makes hosting gatherings a delight, blurring the lines between hospitality and everyday living.

The practical benefits of barndominiums further underscore their appeal. Durability and ease of maintenance are essential to their design, owing to robust materials that withstand the rigors of time and use. Metal roofing, for instance, offers remarkable longevity, shielding the home from the elements with minimal need for upkeep. Similarly, the structural framework of barndominiums, often composed of steel, ensures stability and resilience against external stresses. This emphasis on durability translates to a living environment that demands less maintenance, granting homeowners the luxury of time to pursue their passions and enjoy the comforts of their sanctuary.

Sustainability stands at the core of the barndominium ethos, woven into its very architecture and design philosophy. These homes pay homage to the principle of reuse through the transformation of barns and champion the use of recycled and eco-friendly materials in new constructions. Insulation techniques in barndominiums are meticulously planned to maximize energy efficiency, reducing artificial heating and cooling needs. Incorporating large windows and strategically placed skylights further harnesses natural light, minimizing the reliance on artificial lighting during the day. For those inclined toward self-sufficiency, barndominiums offer the perfect infrastructure to integrate renewable energy sources, such as solar panels, into their design. This commitment to sustainable living mitigates the home's environmental footprint and aligns with the growing consciousness toward responsible stewardship of the planet.

In the narrative of modern architecture, barndominiums emerge as heroes, championing a design ethos that marries aesthetics with functionality. Their appeal lies not just in the tangible attributes of durability, space efficiency, and sustainability but in the intangible quality of versatility they offer. Homeowners can mold their spaces to reflect their journeys, values, and visions for the future. In this light, barndominiums transcend their physical form to become vessels of individual expression and havens of inspired living.

BARNDOMINIUMS VS. TRADITIONAL HOMES: A COST AND LIFESTYLE COMPARISON

In the matrix of modern living, the choice between barndominiums and traditional homes is more than a matter of bricks versus beams; it reflects one's philosophy, a declaration of financial savvy, and an embrace of a lifestyle that defies the cookie-cutter existence. As the scales tip in favor of more personalized, sustainable living spaces, the barndominium emerges as an alternative and a formidable contender in home ownership.

Upfront Costs

The financial gateway to owning a barndominium presents a more manageable threshold than traditional homes. The initial outlay required to bring a barndominium to life, whether through the conversion of an existing structure or the erection of a new one, invariably skews lower. This discrepancy in cost can be attributed to several factors, including the efficiency of using pre-engineered kits and the elimination of complex, costly architectural elements often associated with conventional homes. Additionally, the ability to phase construction allows homeowners to spread expenses over time, making the financial burden more manageable. In contrast, the purchase or construction of traditional homes typically entails a substantial upfront investment driven by higher material costs and labor charges, compounded by the premium on architectural design and customization.

Long-Term Savings

Beyond the initial investment, barndominiums continue to offer financial reprieve through potential savings on utilities, maintenance, and renovations. The architectural DNA of barndominiums, emphasizing open spaces and minimalistic design, lends itself to energy efficiency. Large windows and strategically placed skylights reduce the reliance on artificial lighting, while advanced insulation techniques ensure optimal thermal regulation, curtailing heating and cooling expenses. The materials employed in barndominium construction, known for their durability, demand less in terms of upkeep, allowing homeowners to sidestep the frequent, costly maintenance that often accompanies traditional homes. Furthermore, the innate flexibility of barndominium designs facilitates future modifications or expansions without the need for extensive, disruptive renovations.

Lifestyle Alignment

Its resonance with contemporary lifestyle aspirations is at the heart of the barndominium's appeal. In an era where the clamor for simplicity, sustainability, and personalization grows louder, these structures embody these ideals. The minimalist code that barndominiums adopt, through their open, uncluttered spaces, offers a blank canvas for homeowners to imprint their personal aesthetic and functional preferences, creating environments that reflect their true selves. This capacity for customization goes beyond mere aesthetics, allowing for the creation of spaces that support sustainable living practices, from integrating renewable energy sources to establishing home gardens. The lifestyle offered by barndominiums is one of intentional living, where every square foot serves a purpose, every design element tells a story, and every day is lived in alignment with one's values.

Community Perception

The trajectory of barndominiums within the fabric of real estate and community landscapes is marked by gradual acceptance and growing admiration. Once viewed with skepticism, these structures have steadily gained recognition for their aesthetic appeal, financial advantages, and their role in fostering closer community ties. In areas where traditional homes dominate, barndominiums introduce diversity in housing options, attracting a demographic that values creativity, sustainability, and community engagement. This influx of like-minded individuals can invigorate communities, sparking initiatives aimed at environmental stewardship and collective well-being. Moreover, as barndominiums continue to carve their niche in the housing market, their valuation and desirability have seen a notable uptick, challenging outdated perceptions and cementing their place as viable, valuable living spaces.

In this landscape of evolving housing preferences, barndominiums stand out as symbols of innovation, embodying a blend of financial sensibility, aesthetic versatility, and lifestyle alignment that traditional homes often struggle to match. The choice between the two transcends mere architectural preference, touching on deeper themes of identity, community, and environmental consciousness. As society moves toward a future where the essence of home is defined by more than its physical boundaries, barndominiums offer a vision of living spaces that are not only built for today but are adaptable for the unknowns of tomorrow.

THE SUSTAINABILITY EDGE: ECO-FRIENDLY ASPECTS OF BARNDOMINIUM LIVING

In the evolving narrative of residential architecture, the barndominium emerges not merely as a structure but as a beacon of sustainable living. Its very essence, rooted in the pragmatic reuse of existing barns and the judicious selection of materials, sets a foundation for an environmentally conscious lifestyle that resonates deeply with the spirit of the modern homeowner. This commitment to sustainability extends through every facet of barndominium life, from the inception of its design to the daily practices of its inhabitants, weaving a tapestry of eco-friendliness that distinguishes these homes in the realm of green living.

The architectural genesis of barndominiums in converting barns into living spaces inherently reduces the environmental footprint of new constructions. This adaptive reuse preserves the cultural and structural heritage of the barns while minimizing the demand for raw materials and the energy typically expended in the construction process. For new builds, the preference leans toward materials that are either recycled or sourced with minimal impact on the environment. Steel, a popular choice for barndominium frames, offers the dual advantage of being both durable and recyclable, thus embodying sustainability principles from the ground up. Moreover, the insulation materials favored in barndominium construction, such as spray foam, excel in sealing homes from thermal leaks, enhancing energy conservation while utilizing products that have a lesser impact on the planet.

The design of barndominiums inherently champions energy efficiency, a testament to the ingenuity that marries form with function in the pursuit of eco-friendly living. The expansive windows that hallmark these homes serve a dual purpose, flooding the interior with natural light to reduce reliance on artificial illumination while offering insulation to maintain internal temperatures, thus reducing heating and cooling demands. Similarly, the high ceilings, often left exposed, add to the aesthetic charm and promote air circulation, contributing to a natural cooling effect during warmer months. The strategic orientation of barndominiums, considering the sun's path, further underscores this commitment to energy efficiency, ensuring that homes are warmed by the winter sun while shaded during the peak of summer.

For those dwelling within these structures, the barndominium lifestyle offers ample opportunities to extend their sustainability practices. Integrating solar panels on the expansive roof areas transforms these homes into power generators capable of harnessing the sun's bounty to meet energy needs with minimal environmental impact. Rainwater harvesting systems, easily incorporated into the barndominium design, provide an eco-friendly solution to water consumption, reducing the demand for municipal supplies and minimizing runoff. Inside, the choice of appliances and fixtures mirrors this green philosophy, with homeowners opting for options that conserve water and reduce energy consumption, from low-flow toilets and showerheads to energy-efficient lighting and HVAC (Heating, Ventilation, and Air Conditioning) systems.

Pursuing green certification for a barndominium is an accolade and a testament to the homeowner's dedication to sustainable living. Programs like LEED (Leadership in Energy and Environmental Design) offer a framework through which barndominiums can be evaluated and recognized for their environmental performance and sustainable design. The benefits of such certification extend beyond the personal satisfaction of contributing to the planet's wellbeing; they also encompass the tangible advantages of reduced utility costs and enhanced indoor environmental quality, contributing to a healthier living space. Furthermore, obtaining green certification encourages homeowners to scrutinize every aspect of their home, from construction techniques to daily practices, ensuring that sustainability is woven into their lives.

In this light, barndominiums are not mere residential structures but embodiments of a sustainable future. Their popularity underscores a collective shift toward environmental stewardship, reflecting a growing awareness of personal choices' impact on the world. Through their construction, design, and the lifestyle they foster, barndominiums offer a blueprint for living that harmonizes with the planet, paving the way for a legacy of sustainability that transcends generations.

UNDERSTANDING YOUR BARNDOMINIUM AUDIENCE: WHO IS BUILDING AND WHY?

The tapestry of individuals and families gravitating toward barndominium living paints a vivid picture of diversity, each thread interwoven with unique aspirations, challenges, and dreams. This broad spectrum spans eager millennials stepping into their first homeownership venture to seasoned retirees curating a nest for the golden years. The allure of barndominiums knows no age boundary, appealing equally to young professionals seeking a bespoke living space as it does to families yearning for a haven where they can grow and thrive.

In dissecting the motivations steering this diverse demographic toward barndominiums, a constellation of drivers emerges, each distinct yet universally resonant. Foremost among these is the quest for affordability, a beacon for many in an era where traditional homeownership increasingly slips through the societal grasp. However, the economic pragmatism of barndominiums does not sacrifice the altar of aesthetic and personal expression but amplifies it. This blend of cost-effectiveness with the freedom of customization speaks volumes to those who have long sought a sanctuary that mirrors their individuality without financial strain.

Equally compelling is the narrative of sustainability that barndominiums champion, a testament to the growing consciousness around living in harmony with our planet. This narrative resonates deeply with those who view homes as shelters and extensions of their ethical and environmental values. The ability to reduce one's carbon footprint through adaptive reuse of structures or the integration of green technologies into the fabric of one's living space is appealing—it's becoming a nonnegotiable for a growing segment of the barndominium audience.

Others are motivated by the pursuit of distinct lifestyle objectives that barndominiums skillfully cater to. The minimalist seeking simplicity finds solace in the open, uncluttered spaces that define these homes, spaces that breathe freedom and foster a sense of tranquility. For the remote worker, the barndominium evolves into a dual sanctuary of productivity and rest, where work-life balance is an ideal and a daily reality. The hobby farmer, meanwhile, discovers in the expansive lands that often accompany barndominiums a fertile ground for sustainable living practices, from organic gardening to animal husbandry, weaving a closer bond with the rhythms of nature.

Yet, one of the most intriguing aspects of barndominium living lies in its duality of fostering community and solitude. On the one hand, these structures offer a blueprint for creating tight-knit communities, spaces where shared values around sustainability, creativity, and innovation blossom into communal endeavors. Neighbors become collaborators, working together on community gardens, shared energy projects, or local marketplaces, crafting homes and interconnected lives. This communal spirit does not infringe upon the sanctity of personal space and solitude but enhances it. The barndominium, with its generous expanses, allows for retreats into one's sanctuary, spaces where silence and solitude are treasured companions. This balance, this seamless dance between community engagement and personal retreat, endears barndominiums to such a broad audience, offering a living experience as dynamic as it is serene.

As we navigate the landscape of modern living, the barndominium stands as a beacon of possibility, appealing to a broad audience through its promise of affordability, customization, sustainability, and a lifestyle that harmonizes personal aspirations with communal well-being.

This appeal cuts across demographic lines, drawing in millennials, retirees, families, singles, remote workers, and hobby farmers. Each finds in the barndominium a reflection of their dreams and a foundation for their future. In this sense, the barndominium is more than a home; it is a manifestation of a collective yearning for a living space that is not just built but deeply felt, a space that encompasses the full spectrum of human experience, from the joy of community to the peace of solitude.

BARNDOMINIUMS THROUGH THE AGES: A HISTORICAL PERSPECTIVE

The seed of what we now recognize as the barndominium sprouted in the fertile ground of necessity, in the vast, open fields of agriculture where the boundary between home and workplace was as thin as a barn's wooden slat. Initially, functional agricultural buildings served dual purposes with unpretentious simplicity, housing the hardworking farmer and their equally industrious livestock under one sturdy roof. This early incarnation, while lacking in modern amenities and design, laid the foundational culture of the barndominium: efficiency, simplicity, and a deep connection to the land.

As the decades unfurled, the economic landscape shifted beneath the feet of rural and urban dwellers alike, necessitating a reevaluation of living spaces and their purposes. The Great Depression, followed by post-war booms and subsequent recessions, propelled society to seek cost-effective, multifunctional housing solutions. Barndominiums, with their established attributes of affordability and adaptability, began to evolve, reflecting these economic waves. The once purely utilitarian spaces started incorporating more domestic features, slowly transforming into the contemporary residences we recognize today. This metamorphosis was not merely a change in physical structure but a reflection of a broader cultural trend toward valuing versatility and sustainability in living spaces.

Parallel to these economic and cultural shifts, technological advancements played a pivotal role in reshaping barndominiums. The advent of prefabricated metal buildings in the mid-twentieth century marked a significant leap forward, offering a durable, cost-effective alternative to traditional wooden barns. This innovation extended the lifespan of these structures and expanded their design possibilities, moving away from the conventional rustic aesthetic to embrace a more modern, industrial look. Advanced insulation materials and techniques further enhanced the livability of barndominiums, making them more energy-efficient and suitable for diverse climates. The digital age brought sophisticated design software, allowing for precise customization and visualization of barndominium projects before a single nail was hammered. These technological leaps and a growing DIY culture democratized the creation of barndominiums, making them accessible to a broader audience with varied needs and visions.

Landmark barndominium projects dot the landscape, each serving as a milestone in the concept's evolution and a testament to its growing popularity. One such project, nestled in the rolling hills of Texas, emerged in the late 1990s as a forerunner of the barndominium's potential. This structure, a deft blend of rustic charm and modern functionality, featured expansive open spaces that flowed seamlessly into cozy, private nooks, encapsulating the essence of barndominium living. Its success captured the imagination of a nation, spotlighting the barndominium as a viable, desirable alternative to traditional housing. Another notable example, situated on the outskirts of a bustling Midwestern city, redefined luxury within the context of a barndominium. In the early 2000s, this barndominium boasted high-end finishes, state-of-the-art technology, and eco-friendly features, challenging the perception that barndominiums were merely cost-effective solutions lacking sophistication. These projects, among others, played a pivotal role in popularizing the concept, each serving as a beacon, guiding more individuals toward embracing the barndominium lifestyle.

The historical trajectory of barndominiums, from their humble beginnings to their current status as coveted homes, mirrors the evolving priorities and aspirations of those seeking a place to call home. This evolution, fueled by economic necessity, cultural shifts, and technological advancements, has propelled barndominiums from the sidelines of housing options into the spotlight. As society grapples with issues of sustainability, affordability, and personalization, the barndominium stands ready, a testament to the enduring appeal of living spaces that are as versatile and resilient as the lives they contain.

THE FUTURE OF BARNDOMINIUMS: TRENDS AND INNOVATIONS

In the evolving narrative of architectural design and living spaces, barndominiums stand poised at the cusp of innovation, ready to adapt and flourish amid the shifting sands of aesthetics, sustainability, regulations, and lifestyle dynamics. These structures' inherent flexibility and resilience, combined with a growing societal emphasis on personalization and eco-conscious living, suggest a vibrant and transformative future for barndominiums.

Design Trends

The aesthetic horizon of barndominiums is expanding, driven by a junction of technological advancements and a deepening appreciation for design diversity. Shortly, materials that bond durability with environmental stewardship will become more prevalent. Composite materials, known for their strength and sustainability, alongside reclaimed wood and metal, promise to redefine the textural and visual landscape of barndominiums. These materials contribute to a richer aesthetic palette and echo the growing demand for homes that reflect a commitment to the planet.

Simultaneously, the internal layouts of barndominiums are evolving to accommodate a broader range of lifestyles and activities. Multifunctional spaces, equipped with movable walls and convertible furniture, will cater to the dynamic needs of inhabitants, from remote work to hobbies and entertainment. This fluidity in design, highlighted by an emphasis on natural light and connection with the outdoors, encapsulates the future of living spaces that are both adaptable and centered on well-being.

Smart home technologies embed themselves further into the fabric of barndominiums, enhancing convenience, energy efficiency, and security. Integrated systems that manage everything from lighting and temperature to security and entertainment, all controllable from a smartphone or voice command, will become the norm. This integration of technology not only elevates the living experience but also aligns with the broader trend toward homes that are more responsive and attuned to the needs of their occupants.

Sustainability Innovations

The trajectory of sustainability within barndominiums is marked by both continuity and innovation. Advances in sustainable construction techniques, such as modular building methods that reduce waste and improve efficiency, are set to play a pivotal role. Combined with the increasing use of renewable energy sources like solar and wind, these methods promise to propel barndominiums toward greater self-sufficiency and environmental harmony.

Water conservation technologies, including greywater recycling systems and rainwater harvesting, are expected to become standard features, reflecting a holistic approach to sustainability beyond energy use. The landscaping around barndominiums, too, will embrace sustainability, with native plants and xeriscaping, which emphasizes drought-tolerant plants and minimal water usage, gaining prominence, further reducing water usage and enhancing biodiversity.

Green certifications like LEED and Passive House will likely become more sought after. These certifications serve as benchmarks for sustainability and influence design and construction choices. These certifications validate the environmental credentials of barndominiums and encourage continuous innovation in sustainable living practices.

Regulatory and Market Changes

The regulations and market dynamics surrounding barndominiums are in flux, with potential changes that could significantly impact how and where these structures are built. Building codes and zoning laws, increasingly aware of the unique attributes of barndominiums, may evolve to accommodate these structures better, smoothing the path for their construction and customization. In tandem with the growing recognition of barndominiums within real estate markets, this regulatory evolution suggests a future where these homes are accepted and embraced as valued and viable living spaces.

Market dynamics, influenced by shifting consumer preferences and economic factors, are likely to further cement the place of barndominiums within the housing landscape. As demand for more personalized, sustainable, and cost-effective homes grows, so will the availability and diversity of barndominium offerings, from DIY kits to custom-designed projects. This shift not only broadens the accessibility of barndominiums but also encourages innovation in design, construction, and financing options.

Community and Lifestyle Shifts

The future of barndominiums is essentially linked to evolving lifestyles and work patterns, with these structures offering unique adaptability to the changing contours of daily life. For instance, the rise of remote work underscores the need for homes to integrate professional and personal spaces seamlessly. Barndominiums, with their spacious layouts and potential for customization, are ideally suited to this blending of work and home life, offering dedicated areas for productivity alongside comfortable, inviting living spaces.

Moreover, the growing emphasis on community and shared experiences, accelerated by digital connectivity and shifting social norms, suggests a future where barndominiums serve as nodes within more extensive communal living and collaboration networks. From co-living arrangements to community gardens and shared workshops, barndominiums could play a central role in fostering a sense of belonging and mutual support among residents.

In this dynamic landscape, barndominiums stand as predecessors of a future where homes are not just places of shelter but reflections of individuality, stewards of the environment, and catalysts for the community. As we navigate the unfolding chapters of architectural innovation and lifestyle evolution, barndominiums promise to be at the forefront, embodying the aspirations and values of a society in motion.

2

PLANNING YOUR BARNDOMINIUM PROJECT

The inception of a barndominium project, parallel to planting a seed in fertile soil, demands not just a vision but a strategic approach to nurturing that vision into reality. Brimming with possibilities, this initial phase also beckons a systematic pathway to sift through the myriad of choices, aligning dreams with tangible outcomes.

SETTING YOUR VISION: DEFINING GOALS FOR YOUR BARNDOMINIUM

Clarifying Objectives

The cornerstone of any successful project lies in the clarity of its objectives. Just as an architect meticulously drafts a blueprint, outlining every dimension and detail, so must you delineate the contours of your vision. This vision entails more than a mere wish list; it's an exercise in precision, defining what your barndominium should embody.

Consider aspects such as the scale of the building, the intended use of each space, and how these spaces interact with one another. Reflect on the lifestyle your barndominium is to facilitate—is it a haven of tranquility, a hub of creativity, or a blend of both?

Design Preferences

Navigating through the vast expanse of design aesthetics can seem daunting. Yet, this exploration is crucial in carving out a space that resonates with your style. You can start by immersing yourself in a variety of design paradigms. Architecture blogs or platforms like Pinterest serve as reservoirs of inspiration, offering a glimpse into the myriad ways barndominiums can be styled. Whether you gravitate toward the rustic charm of exposed beams and natural wood or the sleek minimalism of modern design, identify elements that speak to you. This process not only hones your design preferences but also illuminates how these choices reflect your lifestyle and values.

Functionality and Future-Proofing

A home is more than a static environment; it's a dynamic space that evolves in tandem with its occupants. Anticipating future needs and ensuring the adaptability of your barndominium is paramount. Designing rooms that can transition from a home office to a nursery or incorporating accessibility features is paramount. Consider the inevitable technological advancements and how they might integrate into your home. Planning for flexibility ensures your barndominium remains a fitting backdrop to your life, accommodating shifts with grace.

Vision Board Creation

Crafting a vision board, whether physically with cut-outs and a poster board or digitally using tools like Canva, is a tangible manifestation of your aspirations. This collage of images, materials, textures, and colors is a source of inspiration and a visual guide that aligns your project with your initial vision. It's a reference point that communicates your aesthetic and functional desires to architects, designers, and builders, ensuring everyone shares a cohesive understanding of the project's direction.

Step-by-Step Guide to Creating Your Digital Vision Board

1. **Collect Inspiration:** Spend time gathering images that capture the essence of your desired barndominium, focusing on architecture, interior design, landscaping, and any other relevant elements.
2. **Choose a Platform:** Select a digital tool like Canva or Pinterest to assemble your vision board. Both platforms offer intuitive interfaces and a wealth of resources to craft your board.
3. **Organize Your Board:** Create sections for different aspects of your project—exteriors, interiors, materials, and so forth. This organization aids in maintaining clarity and focus.
4. **Refine Your Selection:** As your board takes shape, refine your choices to ensure they align with your clarified objectives and design preferences.

5. **Share and Discuss:** Use your vision board as a communication tool. Share it with your project team to discuss its feasibility, gather feedback, and ensure your vision is understood.

This interactive exercise solidifies your vision and fosters collaboration, ensuring the project evolves from a personal dream into a shared endeavor.

In navigating the initial stages of planning your barndominium, remember that this phase is as much about dreaming as it is about grounding those dreams in reality. It's a delicate balance between aspiration and pragmatism, guided by a clear understanding of your objectives, a keen eye for design, thoughtful consideration of future needs, and a collaborative spirit. With these pillars in place, the foundation for your barndominium project stands ready to support the magnificent structure it is destined to become.

BUDGETING BASICS: PLANNING YOUR FINANCES FROM START TO FINISH

Cost Estimation

In creating your barndominium, the initial step involves crafting an intricate tapestry of financial predictions, weaving together various cost elements to form a coherent picture of your project's financial demands. This venture begins with acquiring land, a foundational expense that sets the stage for all subsequent financial planning. The cost of land varies widely, influenced by location, size, and accessibility, necessitating a diligent search and negotiation process to secure a parcel that aligns with your vision and budget. Following this, construction costs emerge as the next pillar of financial estimation. Here, the spectrum ranges from the expense of laying a robust foundation to the intricate details of interior finishes. Each choice, from the materials for your walls to the bathrooms' fixtures, carries a financial weight, requiring meticulous consideration and selection. Additionally, the hidden costs, often overlooked, such as permits, utility connections, and landscaping, must be accounted for, ensuring a comprehensive financial blueprint that leaves no stone unturned.

Funding Options

Navigating the landscape of financial procurement for your barndominium project introduces a plethora of avenues, each with its own merits and considerations. Traditional mortgages, a standard route for many homeowners, may present challenges due to the unique nature of barndominiums, prompting a need for creative financing solutions. Construction loans emerge as a viable alternative, offering the flexibility to draw funds incrementally throughout the build process. This option, however, demands a detailed project plan and budget, alongside a willingness to adhere to the lender's oversight and disbursement schedule. For those seeking a path less trodden, alternative financing options such as peer-to-peer lending platforms or tapping into personal savings offer a degree of autonomy and flexibility not found in traditional lending. These routes, while freeing, require a heightened level of financial discipline and risk management to ensure the viability of your project from inception to completion.

Budget Management

Managing your budget throughout your barndominium project can be compared to navigating a ship through the unpredictable waters of financial uncertainty. Adapting to unforeseen costs requires a steadfast commitment to fiscal discipline and agility. Implementing a system of rigorous bookkeeping, where every expense is meticulously logged and categorized, forms the backbone of effective budget management. This practice, when paired with regular reviews of financial progress against the initial budget, illuminates areas of overspending or savings, allowing for timely adjustments. Contingency planning, an often underappreciated aspect of budget management, involves setting aside a portion of your budget to address unexpected expenses. Typically, a 10–20 percent contingency fund of your total budget acts as a financial buffer, ensuring unforeseen costs do not derail your project. Additionally, employing cost-saving strategies such as sourcing materials directly from manufacturers or opting for slightly used or refurbished items can stretch your budget further, allowing for allocating funds to areas of higher priority or impact.

Financial Pitfalls to Avoid

The financial journey of bringing a barndominium to life is fraught with pitfalls that can trap the unwary, leading to budgetary overruns and project delays. A common misstep involves underestimating the actual construction and finishing cost, a miscalculation from inadequate research, or overly optimistic cost projections. This oversight can lead to a financial shortfall, forcing compromises on critical aspects of the project or, in extreme cases, halting construction altogether. Similarly, the allure of non-essential features and upgrades can seduce one into diverting funds from crucial components of the build, compromising the integrity and functionality of the final structure. Succumbing to the charm of the latest technological marvels or luxury finishes without a precise evaluation of their necessity or long-term value often results in financial regret. Another hidden danger lies in neglecting the allocation of funds for post-construction expenses such as furniture, appliances, and landscaping, which transform a structure into a home. Recognizing and steering clear of these financial pitfalls through diligent planning, disciplined budgeting, and a focus on the essentials ensures the smooth realization of your barndominium dream, safeguarding against the financial strains that tarnish the joy of creating your ideal living space.

NAVIGATING ZONING LAWS AND BUILDING PERMITS

Understanding Zoning Laws

In the labyrinth of constructing a barndominium, the intricacies of local zoning laws emerge as crucial navigational beacons. These regulations, often as varied as the landscapes they govern, dictate the permissible uses of land within specific jurisdictions, influencing not merely the feasibility but the foundation of your barndominium project. Grasping the nuances of these laws becomes imperative as they define the constraints and freedoms in the design, location, and function of your envisioned home. Zoning laws delve into specifics such as minimum lot size, building height, and the proportion of land a structure can cover, each parameter shaping the potential of your barndominium to align with your aspirations. This understanding prevents costly missteps and unveils opportunities to optimize your design within the legal framework, ensuring that your project not only dreams big but stands tall.

Permit Process

The acquisition of building permits is a rite of passage for your barndominium project, a formal nod from authorities that transforms plans into actionable blueprints. While meticulous, this process is a safeguard, ensuring that your construction adheres to local building codes and standards, guaranteeing safety and compliance. Initiating this journey requires a comprehensive dossier encompassing detailed construction plans, site surveys, and, often, evidence of approval from environmental and other regulatory bodies. Navigating this terrain demands patience and precision as the documentation undergoes scrutiny and is subject to queries and revisions. Potential obstacles—requests for additional details, modifications to meet codes, or delays in review times—call for proactive engagement and a readiness to adapt. This phase, though daunting, is pivotal, laying the groundwork for a project that not only meets legal standards but also embodies the vision of safety and harmony with its surroundings.

Working with Local Authorities

Fostering a cooperative relationship with local authorities transcends mere courtesy; it becomes a strategic alliance that facilitates the smooth progression of your barndominium project. Engaging early and often with zoning and building departments, armed with well-prepared documentation and a respectful understanding of their role in safeguarding community standards, establishes a foundation of mutual respect and collaboration. This dialogue, characterized by transparency and responsiveness, can expedite the review process and unearth constructive feedback, guiding necessary adjustments with clarity and efficiency. Moreover, this proactive engagement demystifies the regulatory landscape, transforming what might seem like bureaucratic hurdles into manageable steps toward realizing your dream home. The essence of this interaction lies not in negotiation but in partnership, recognizing that the authorities are not gatekeepers but guides on your path to compliance and safety.

Case Studies

The journey from conception to completion of a barndominium is laden with tales of triumph over regulatory challenges, each offering unique insights and encouragement. One such story unfolds in the heart of a rural county, where a family's dream of converting a historic barn into a modern living space faced the twin challenges of stringent historic preservation codes and modern building standards. Through diligent research, open dialogue with local authorities, and a flexible design approach, they navigated these regulations, preserving the barn's historic facade while incorporating contemporary safety and energy efficiency standards. Their success lay in viewing regulations not as constraints but as a framework within which to craft a home that honored its heritage while embracing the future.

Another narrative highlights an urban couple aspiring to erect a barndominium in a predominantly residential area, where zoning laws were tightly knit around traditional housing. The couple's strategy involved a thorough presentation of their project to the zoning board, highlighting how their design, though unconventional, adhered to the aesthetic and functional standards of the community. Supplementing their proposal with testimonials from architects and engineers, they demonstrated their commitment to safety, sustainability, and community harmony. Their eventual victory was a testament to the power of preparation, persuasion, and the willingness to engage openly with regulatory bodies, setting a precedent for future barndominium projects within the community.

These case studies, each a mosaic of challenges, strategies, and triumphs, serve as beacons for aspiring barndominium owners. They underscore the importance of understanding and navigating zoning laws and permits, not as mere administrative tasks but as integral steps in the dance of bringing your dream home to life. Through meticulous planning, proactive engagement, and a spirit of collaboration, the path through the regulatory landscape becomes navigable and a journey of discovery, revealing the potential to create a home that respects its legal and community context while boldly reflecting your vision and values.

CHOOSING THE RIGHT LOCATION: WHAT TO CONSIDER

The quest for the ideal parcel of land on which to erect a barndominium is not merely a prelude to construction but a decisive factor influencing every facet of the project's execution and eventual habitation. This initial decision, seemingly straightforward, is imbued with complexity, requiring a careful appraisal of various parameters that extend beyond mere aesthetics to encompass practical, environmental, and lifestyle considerations.

Land Selection Criteria

At the heart of this deliberation lies the imperative of location, a multifaceted criterion that encompasses more than geographic desirability. It's a balance between accessibility and seclusion, where the proximity to urban conveniences must be weighed against the tranquility of rural expanses. The land's topography further complicates this equation, introducing variables such as elevation, slope, and natural features that can either enhance or impede the vision for the barndominium. A gently sloping hill might offer panoramic views and natural drainage but could also escalate construction costs and complexity. Likewise, access to utilities, often taken for granted in urban settings, becomes a pivotal consideration, dictating the feasibility of connecting to electrical grids, water supply, and sewer systems and influencing long-term living costs and sustainability efforts.

Impact of Location on Design

The chosen locale profoundly influences the architectural blueprint and structural elements of a barndominium. Orientation, a critical location aspect, is pivotal in harnessing natural light, optimizing thermal comfort, and framing views that transform living spaces. A site's orientation toward the sun's path mitigates energy consumption by maximizing daylight and enhancing passive solar heating but also defines the interaction between indoor and outdoor spaces, blurring the boundaries with nature. The topographical nuances of the location further inform design decisions, from integrating the barndominium into the landscape to mitigating environmental challenges such as wind exposure and water runoff. Thus, the symbiosis between location and design becomes a dance of adaptation, where architectural creativity meets the inherent attributes of the land.

Environmental Considerations

In the stewardship of constructing a barndominium, environmental considerations take precedence, guiding the selection process with an eye toward sustainability and resilience. Soil quality emerges as a critical determinant, influencing the foundation's integrity and the potential for agricultural endeavors and landscaping ambitions. A thorough soil assessment can unveil challenges such as poor drainage or susceptibility to erosion, necessitating adjustments in design or site preparation. Evaluating flood risk is equally critical, a parameter that balances inconvenience against safety, insurance implications, and long-term property value. Selecting a site with a minimal flood risk or taking preemptive measures to mitigate such risk safeguards the investment and the future feasibility of the barndominium as a haven.

Community and Lifestyle

The confluence of community and lifestyle aspirations with the choice of location encapsulates a broader reflection on the desired quality of life. For some, the allure of a barndominium is closely linked to the prospect of rural solitude, offering an escape from the noise of urban life where the natural rhythms govern the pace of living. Here, selecting a remote locale, entrenched in the serenity of the countryside, resonates with aspirations for simplicity, self-sufficiency, and a profound connection to the land. Conversely, others may seek a harmonious blend of country charm and community engagement, opting for locations within or near established neighborhoods. This proximity fosters a sense of belonging, offering opportunities for social interaction, community involvement, and easy access to amenities and services. Thus, the choice of location reflects one's lifestyle philosophy, a deliberate selection that aligns the physical setting of the barndominium with the envisioned way of life.

In the tapestry of planning a barndominium, selecting the perfect location is a thread that weaves through the fabric of the entire project, influencing design, construction, and inhabitation. This decision, approached with diligence and foresight, lays the groundwork for a home that not only stands as a testament to architectural beauty and functionality but also harmonizes with the environment and echoes the values and aspirations of those who dwell within its walls.

DESIGNING YOUR FLOOR PLAN: TIPS FOR EFFICIENCY AND AESTHETICS

Crafting a floor plan is a pivotal phase in constructing a barndominium. It intertwines the threads of efficiency and aesthetics into a coherent whole. Far from mere technicality, this art form harmonizes space dynamics with the homeowner's personal touch, ensuring every square inch serves both function and form.

Maximizing Space

The optimization of space within the confines of a floor plan requires an acute understanding of the multifaceted nature of rooms and their potential to serve dual or multiple purposes. Envisioning rooms that adapt to the evolving needs of their occupants without sacrificing comfort or style necessitates a strategic approach. Incorporating elements such as fold-away furniture, built-in storage solutions, and adaptable room dividers can transform a static area into a dynamic space capable of hosting a quiet study session one moment and a vibrant gathering the next. The key lies in anticipating these shifting needs, embedding flexibility into the very architecture of the barndominium. Smartly positioned storage options, cleverly designed to meld seamlessly with the interior decor, further enhance this fluidity, ensuring that practical necessities do not compromise the aesthetics of the space.

Aesthetic Harmony

Achieving a symbiotic relationship between the barndominium's exterior and interior design necessitates a delicate balance, a dance between the building's architectural integrity and the personal style of its inhabitants. This harmony is not merely about color schemes or material choices but the seamless transition between the home's external presence and internal atmosphere. It is crucial to consider how exterior architectural features, such as large windows or expansive doors, influence the interior light and space and how these elements can accentuate or soften the transition between outside and inside. Materials play a pivotal role in this regard, with complementary textures and elements that echo the home's external character within its interior spaces, fostering continuity and flow. Thoughtfully designed outdoor living areas reflect the interior design motifs, further blurring the boundaries between inside and out, extending the living space, and enhancing the overall aesthetic appeal.

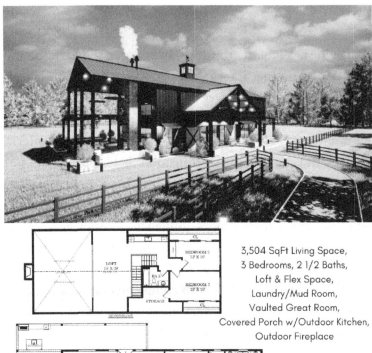

3,504 SqFt Living Space,
3 Bedrooms, 2 1/2 Baths,
Loft & Flex Space,
Laundry/Mud Room,
Vaulted Great Room,
Covered Porch w/Outdoor Kitchen,
Outdoor Fireplace

Personalization and Flexibility

The essence of a barndominium lies not just in its structural form but also in its ability to encapsulate the unique identity of its owners. Therefore, personalization in the design process is not a mere option but a necessity, allowing the space to mirror the individuality and style of those who dwell within. This personal touch extends beyond decorative choices, embedding itself in the layout and functionality of the floor plan. Rooms designed with adaptability in mind, capable of evolving alongside the changing phases of life, reflect a deep understanding of the transient nature of human needs. This approach ensures that the barndominium remains a true reflection of its occupants, a canvas on which their evolving story is painted.

Incorporating personal artifacts, heirlooms, or bespoke pieces into the design adds a layer of uniqueness and imbues the space with a sense of history and continuity. The challenge lies in balancing these personal elements with the overarching design theme, ensuring the space remains coherent and harmonious. Here, the concept of "flexible design" comes into play, with spaces crafted to be redefined over time, their purpose and appearance shifting in response to the inhabitants' journey.

Professional Collaboration

Translating a vision into a tangible floor plan is a complex process that often necessitates the expertise of professionals who can bridge the gap between dreams and reality. Collaborating with architects and designers is not a relinquishment of control but an embrace of partnership, leveraging their expertise to refine and elevate the initial vision. This collaboration is a dialogue, one in which the homeowner's personal aspirations and practical requirements are melded with professional insights to create a floor plan that is both beautiful and functional.

Selecting the right professional partners requires a discerning eye, looking beyond portfolios to understand their design philosophy, communication style, and willingness to co-create better. The ideal collaborator is one who not only respects the homeowner's vision but is also willing to challenge assumptions and propose innovative solutions that enhance the project's overall design and functionality. This partnership, based on mutual respect and a shared commitment to excellence, ensures that the floor plan of the barndominium not only meets but also exceeds the expectations of those who will call it home.

This intricate process of designing a floor plan, maximizing space, achieving aesthetic harmony, embedding personalization, and fostering professional collaboration forms the cornerstone of creating a barndominium that is not merely a structure but a sanctuary. It is a testament to the power of thoughtful design to transform a blueprint into a living, breathing space that resonates with its inhabitants' warmth, style, and spirit.

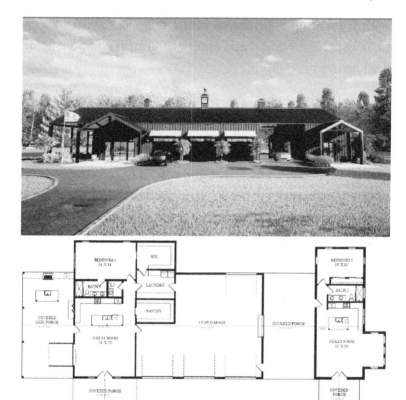

2,900 SqFt Living Space, 1 Bedroom, 1 1/2 Baths, In-Law Suite w/Full Bath, Pass-Thru Kitchen Window Bar & Outdoor Kitchen, Gable Front Porch & Vaulted Covered Side Porch, Glass Garage Door, 3 Bay/5 Car Garage

SELECTING YOUR BARNDOMINIUM BUILDER: A GUIDE TO VETTING PROFESSIONALS

Choosing a builder for your barndominium is a pivotal decision that significantly influences the trajectory of your project. This selection process demands a more nuanced approach, where various criteria are carefully considered to ensure the partnership aligns with your vision, budget, and expectations. The builder becomes a collaborator entrusted with translating your dream into a tangible reality, making their expertise, beliefs, and approach critical components in the journey of creation.

Criteria for Choosing a Builder

In the vast sea of construction professionals, identifying a builder with the right blend of experience, reputation, and communication style becomes your first task. Experience with barndominiums is paramount, as this niche requires a specific understanding of these structures' unique challenges and opportunities. A builder's portfolio, rich with barndominium projects, speaks volumes of their proficiency in navigating the intricacies of such builds, from material selection to the nuances of custom design.

Reputation holds equal weight, serving as a beacon to potential pitfalls or a testament to consistent excellence. Delve into reviews, seek testimonials, and engage with past clients to glean insights into the builder's reliability, quality of work, and adherence to timelines and budgets. This survey offers a glimpse into your experience, illuminating the builder's capacity to meet, if not exceed, your expectations.

Although often overlooked, the subtleties of communication style are crucial in fostering a smooth collaboration. A builder who listens attentively, communicates transparently and responds quickly to questions and concerns not only eases the stress inherent in construction projects but also ensures that your vision is accurately understood and executed. This synergy between client and builder, founded on mutual respect and clear communication, lays the groundwork for a successful partnership.

Interviewing Prospective Builders

Armed with a shortlist of potential builders, the interview process becomes critical in making your final selection. This dialogue is an opportunity to probe deeper into the builder's approach, character, and compatibility with your project. Questions framed around their experience with barndominiums, explicitly asking for examples of challenges faced and how they overcame them, offer insights into their problem-solving skills and adaptability. Inquiries about their materials sourcing, subcontractors, and managing timelines and budgets reveal their operational efficiency and reliability.

Discussing their process for change orders and handling unexpected issues during construction will provide a clear picture of their flexibility and transparency in dealing with the unpredictable nature of building projects. Moreover, understanding their warranty and post-construction support services uncovers their commitment to customer satisfaction and the longevity of their work. This interrogation, conducted with a balance of curiosity and scrutiny, peels back the layers, allowing you to assess the builder's suitability for your barndominium project.

Reviewing Contracts

The contract with your builder is more than a formal agreement; it safeguards your project's success, outlining both parties' expectations, responsibilities, and protections. A thorough review of this document, ideally with legal counsel, ensures that all aspects of the project are clearly defined and agreed upon. Critical elements such as detailed timelines, comprehensive cost breakdowns, and the scope of work offer transparency and accountability, mitigating the risk of misunderstandings or disputes.

Including a detailed change order process within the contract provides a structured approach to managing alterations to the initial plan, ensuring that any modifications are documented, priced, and approved relatively by both the client and builder. Equally important is the clarity around warranty terms, specifying what is covered, for how long, and the process for addressing issues that may arise post-construction. This meticulous examination and negotiation of the contract terms lay a robust foundation for your project, anchored in mutual understanding and legal integrity.

Builder-Client Relationship

The relationship between you and your builder is the cornerstone of your barndominium project's success. Cultivating this relationship requires an investment in open, continuous communication, where expectations are articulated through constructive feedback and challenges are collaboratively addressed. This dynamic, characterized by mutual respect and a shared commitment to the project's success, transforms the construction process into a partnership, where obstacles are navigated with a united front and victories are celebrated jointly.

The essence of this partnership transcends the transactional, fostering an environment where creativity flourishes, solutions emerge, and the journey toward realizing your dream home is marked by milestones of collaboration and achievement. Within this relationship's strength, your barndominium's vision, with all its unique aspirations and intricacies, becomes a reality, crafted not just with bricks and mortar but with trust, expertise, and shared ambition.

SUSTAINABLE BUILDING PRACTICES FOR YOUR BARNDOMINIUM

Green Construction Materials

In the architectural symphony that is a barndominium, the selection of materials plays a pivotal note, resonating through the structure's every inch with implications for its inhabitants and the environment. Opting for green construction materials is not merely an ecological statement but a profound commitment to a sustainable ethos. With its rapid regeneration, bamboo emerges as a sterling flooring choice, offering durability and environmental credentials. Recycled steel, embodying strength and resilience, forms an ideal framework for those seeking to minimize their ecological footprint without compromising structural integrity. Within the walls, sheep's wool insulation presents a natural, efficient alternative to synthetic options, ensuring thermal comfort while fostering healthier indoor air quality. This deliberate choice of materials, each carrying the banner of sustainability, imbues the barndominium with a green heart, setting a foundation that is as environmentally conscious as it is physically enduring.

Energy Efficiency

The quest for energy efficiency within the realm of barndominium construction unfolds as a strategic endeavor where design and innovation converge to minimize consumption while maximizing comfort. The passive solar design stands at the forefront of this effort, a testament to the meticulous alignment of the structure with the sun's arc to harness its warmth in the colder months while deflecting its intensity when the mercury rises. This natural regulation of indoor temperature reduces reliance on mechanical heating and cooling, thus lowering energy usage. High-performance insulation, snug within walls and ceilings, acts as a steadfast guardian against thermal leakage, ensuring the energy used to temper the interior climate is used judiciously. Implementing energy-efficient windows and sealing the envelope against the intrusion of external temperature fluctuations further consolidates the barndominium's energy-efficient stance. These strategies, interwoven within the essence of the design, elevate the barndominium to a pinnacle of energy efficiency, where comfort is achieved with minimal environmental cost.

Water Conservation

Water conservation is a critical theme in sculpting a barndominium that shelters and sustains, echoing through the myriad decisions shaping its creation. Integrating low-flow fixtures in kitchens and bathrooms translates into significant reductions in water usage without diminishing functionality, embodying a simple yet effective step toward sustainability. Rainwater harvesting systems, capturing the bounty of the skies, offer a renewable source for landscaping and non-potable water needs, reducing demand for municipal supplies and forging a deeper connection with the natural water cycle. The landscaping surrounding the barndominium further reflects this spirit, with native plants and xeriscaping requiring minimal irrigation, thus conserving water while enhancing the structure's harmony with its environment. Each one, a drop in the broader ocean of sustainability, these measures collectively form a robust approach to water conservation, ensuring that the barndominium exists within the landscape and actively contributes to its preservation.

Example of Underground Rainwater Harvesting

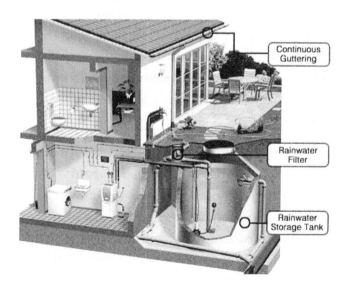

Long-Term Sustainability

The vision of a barndominium, painted with broad strokes of sustainability, reaches beyond the immediate to embrace the future, ensuring that the structure's legacy has a minimal environmental impact and enduring efficiency. The comprehensive adoption of green construction materials, energy-efficient designs, and water-conserving practices lays a foundation that withstands the test of time, both physically and environmentally. This approach not only reduces the barndominium's operational costs, offering financial savings that accrue over the years but also lessens its ecological footprint, contributing to the health and vitality of the planet. Moreover, integrating sustainable practices in the construction and operation of a barndominium sets a precedent, serving as a blueprint for future endeavors and inspiring a broader embrace of eco-conscious living. In this commitment to long-term sustainability, the actual value of a barndominium is realized, not just as a home but as a beacon of environmental stewardship, illuminating a path toward a more sustainable future for all.

In crafting a barndominium, green construction materials, energy efficiency, water conservation, and long-term sustainability intertwine to form a tapestry of ecological responsibility. This deliberate weaving, mindful of both the immediate and the enduring, instills the structure with a depth of purpose that transcends the physical, positioning it as a testament to the possibility of harmonious coexistence with our environment. As we move forward, let us carry these principles with us, allowing them to guide not only the construction of our homes but also the shaping of our lives, fostering a world where sustainability is not just an aspiration but a lived reality.

ONE-YEAR GUIDE TO EFFECTIVELY BUDGET FOR YOUR DREAM BARNDOMINIUM

Adhering to a comprehensive and methodical planning strategy is imperative for effectively allocating financial resources for such an initiative over the course of one year. Presented herein is a one-year guideline designed to assist in budgeting for your barndominium project.

Month 1: Research and Planning

1. **Define Your Vision:** Determine the size, style, and features you want in your barndominium. Consider the number of rooms, bathrooms, and special amenities.
2. **Budget Estimation:** To estimate your initial budget, begin by researching the typical costs of building a barndominium in your area. Consider the cost of materials, labor, and any other services you might need.

Month 2–3: Detailed Budgeting and Financing

1. **Get Detailed Quotes:** Contact contractors and suppliers for detailed quotes. Make sure to get multiple bids to ensure competitive pricing.
2. **Secure Financing:** If you need a loan, this is the time to talk to banks or financial institutions. Compare

different loan offers and choose the one that suits your budget and timeline.

Month 4–6: Finalizing Plans and Permits

1. **Blueprints and Design:** Hire an architect or use pre-designed plans. Finalize your blueprints.
2. **Obtain Permits:** Start obtaining necessary building permits from local authorities.

Month 7–9: Breaking Ground

1. **Site Preparation:** This includes clearing the land, laying foundations, and preparing for utilities.
2. **Begin Construction:** With everything in place, construction can begin. Make sure to regularly check on the progress and quality of work.

Month 10–11: Interior and Exterior Work

1. **Exterior:** Ensure the roofing, siding, and exterior finishes have all been completed.
2. **Interior:** Focus on interior walls, flooring, electricity, plumbing, and HVAC systems. Begin to see the interior take shape.

Month 12: Finishing Touches and Move-In

1. **Final Installations:** Install cabinets, countertops, lighting fixtures, and appliances.
2. **Inspections and Approvals:** Ensure that your

barndominium passes all required inspections before. moving in.

3. **Move-In Preparation:** Plan the move-in process, including purchasing furniture and organizing your belongings.

Throughout the Year: Monitoring and Adjusting the Budget

- **Regular Check-Ins:** Monitor expenses monthly to ensure you are on track with the budget.
- **Contingency Fund:** Always maintain a contingency fund (typically 10–20 percent of the overall budget) to manage unforeseen costs.

Considerations

- **Seasonal Factors:** Weather can affect construction schedules. Plan your construction phase during favorable weather conditions if possible.
- **Quality vs. Cost:** Balancing quality and cost is crucial. Invest in quality where it matters, such as structural integrity and insulation.
- **DIY Opportunities:** Consider what parts of the construction or finishing you can do yourself to save money.

Adhering to this budgeting guide will help ensure your barndominium project is financially manageable and progresses smoothly. Be prepared to adjust your plans as needed, especially when unexpected costs arise.

3

ARCHITECTURAL DESIGN AND AESTHETICS

At the heart of every barndominium lies a story of harmony between the rustic allure of barn living and the sleek, refined lines of modern design. This blend does not come about by happenstance but through deliberate choices in materials, designs, and an understanding of how spaces can convey warmth, functionality, and innovation. The art of merging these seemingly disparate worlds requires a thoughtful approach that respects each style's integrity while seeking a unified aesthetic that speaks to the homeowner's soul.

THE ART OF BLENDING RUSTIC AND MODERN ELEMENTS

The fusion of rustic charm with contemporary design in a barndominium sets the stage for a living space grounded in tradition and soaring with modernity. Achieving this balance is akin to a chef creating a signature dish that marries unexpected flavors in a way that delights yet comforts.

Harmonizing Styles

The key to melding rustic and modern is finding common ground where each style's strengths are celebrated without overshadowing the other. It's about letting the rustic elements tell their story of heritage and endurance while allowing modern touches to introduce a narrative of efficiency and sleekness. For instance, the warmth of reclaimed wood floors can serve as a counterpoint to the coolness of stainless steel appliances, creating a dialogue between materials that enriches the space.

Material Selection

Choosing materials embodying rusticity and modernity is crucial for this harmonious blend. When paired with metal accents or concrete countertops, exposed wood beams, a staple in rustic architecture, bridge the gap between the old and the new. The wood introduces a touch of nature and history, while metal and concrete bring in the clean lines and simplicity favored in modern design. This juxtaposition highlights the beauty of each material and reflects the complex character of the barndominium itself.

Design Techniques

Focus on simplicity and authenticity to balance rustic elements with modern design. A minimalist approach, avoiding clutter and embracing open spaces, allows the materials and craftsmanship to shine. Incorporating large, frameless windows not only floods the space with natural light but also acts as a modern counterbalance to the robust, earthy materials used in rustic design. In areas where indoor and outdoor spaces merge seamlessly, the design cultivates a bond with the natural surroundings, epitomizing the essence of rustic and contemporary styles.

Case Studies

Consider a barndominium where the living room integrates a century-old, rough-hewn barn beam with a polished concrete floor. The contrast is striking yet harmonious, with the beam's texture and history playing off the floor's contemporary feel and durability. Another example is a kitchen where traditional, handcrafted cabinets are set against a backdrop of sleek, stainless steel appliances and minimalist light fixtures. The result is a space that feels rooted yet airy, a testament to the versatility and timeless-ness of combining rustic and modern elements.

Material Mood Board Creation

Creating a mood board effectively visualizes the blend of rustic and modern elements for your barndominium. Start by selecting images of materials, textures, and colors that speak to both styles. Please include examples of wood, metal, concrete, and glass, paying attention to how their qualities complement or contrast each other. You can use an online platform or a physical board to arrange your selections, playing with combinations until you find a balance that resonates with your vision. This exercise not only aids in material selection but also serves as a communication tool with designers and builders, ensuring your vision is conveyed and understood.

In weaving together the rustic and modern, the barndominium becomes more than a structure; it transforms into a testament to the beauty of balanced contrasts. It stands as a reminder that spaces are not just built but crafted with intention, where every beam, every tile, and every pane of glass tells a part of the story—a story of a home that honors its roots while embracing the present and looking forward to the future.

MAXIMIZING SPACE WITH OPEN-CONCEPT LIVING

The allure of open-concept living in a barndominium is not merely a byproduct of contemporary architectural trends but a reflection of a more profound yearning for spaces that foster connection, illuminate with daylight, and flow with an unencumbered grace. This architectural philosophy disavows the traditional segmentation of living areas, opting for a layout where boundaries dissolve, inviting light to meander and conversations to float freely across the home. The benefits of such a design extend beyond the aesthetic, touching upon the very way life unfurls within the walls.

Open-concept plans shine when it comes to enhancing natural light within a barndominium. By removing barriers, sunlight finds no obstacle in its path, casting warmth and luminosity across the vast expanse of the interior. This infusion of daylight elevates the mood and health of those residing within and reduces the reliance on artificial lighting, echoing the deposition of sustainability that often guides the construction of these homes. Furthermore, the architectural choice of expansive windows and strategically placed skylights complements this endeavor, ensuring that from dawn until dusk, every corner of the home basks in a natural glow.

The design of open-concept spaces demands a meticulous approach that balances the freedom of flow with the necessity of function. Here, zoning emerges as a pivotal strategy, distinguishing areas of activity without erecting physical barriers. Strategic placement of furnishings and subtle shifts in flooring materials or ceiling heights can denote the transition from a culinary haven to a serene lounge or a stimulating workspace. This demarcation of zones ensures that, despite the absence of walls, each segment of the barndominium serves its purpose with distinction, whether it be hosting gatherings, culinary adventures, or moments of solitary repose.

Furniture placement within an open-concept barndominium transcends mere decoration, acting instead as a compass that guides movement and interaction. The choice and arrangement of furnishings are instrumental in defining the character of each zone, creating invisible boundaries that intuitively navigate inhabitants through the space. A well-placed sectional sofa can create a cozy, relaxing nook amid a larger living area. At the same time, a robust dining table anchors the dining space, inviting fellowship over meals. The key lies in selecting pieces that resonate with the barndominium's aesthetic, ensuring that each item not only fulfills a functional role but also contributes to the overall harmony of the space.

Integrating private, quiet spaces within the fluidity of an open-concept floor plan presents a unique challenge that requires creativity and a keen understanding of the inhabitants' needs. These sanctuaries of solitude, essential for reflection, work, or rest, can be artfully woven into the broader tapestry of the barndominium without disrupting its open ethos. Sliding barn doors or sleek, retractable panels offer the flexibility to seclude these areas, providing peace without permanence. Similarly, strategically using bookshelves or indoor plants as natural dividers can imbue these private nooks with a sense of enclosure while maintaining a connection to the home's communal spirit.

In open-concept living, the barndominium transforms into a canvas where light dances, spaces breathe, and life unfolds fluidly. This architectural approach does not simply create a house but cultivates a home where every square foot resonates with purpose, every beam basks in sunlight, and every moment is easily shared. Through thoughtful design, strategic zoning, and the artful placement of furniture, the open-concept barndominium emerges as a testament to the beauty of unbounded living, where the only walls that exist are those that bring us together.

INCORPORATING NATURAL LIGHT: TIPS AND TRICKS

In the architectural narrative of a barndominium, the infusion of natural light plays a pivotal role, not just as an aesthetic enhancer but as a vitality-bringing element that transforms spaces into sanctuaries of brightness and warmth. The strategic incorporation of natural light necessitates innovative design features and thoughtful interior choices, each contributing to an ambiance where light enters and enriches the living environment.

Maximizing Natural Light

Architectural features designed to capture and distribute natural light effectively become essential components in the blueprint of a barndominium. Large windows, positioned with precision, act as conduits for sunlight, drawing its energy into the heart of the home. These glass panes, expansive and often stretching from floor to ceiling, blur the boundary between the interior and the exterior, inviting the landscape in and allowing light to roam freely across rooms. Skylights, another architectural marvel, open the ceiling to the sky, channeling daylight downward and illuminating spaces that windows might not reach. Their placement, especially in communal areas or dark corridors, transforms these spaces, introducing an element of the outdoors inside. The adoption of sliding glass doors not only enhances accessibility to outdoor living areas but also serves as a medium for light, ensuring that even the transition spaces bask in the glow of natural illumination.

3,140 SqFt Living Space,
4 Bedrooms, 3 Baths,
Pantry/Laundry,
Outdoor Fireplace,
Glass Garage Door,
Pass-Thru Kitchen Window Bar

Orientation and Design

The orientation of a barndominium is a critical factor in optimizing natural light, a consideration that begins at the site selection phase and extends through to the final design. An alignment that takes advantage of the sun's trajectory, positioning living spaces toward the south in northern hemispheres, ensures that these areas receive a generous amount of sunlight throughout the day. This strategic orientation, coupled with the thoughtful placement of windows and skylights, maximizes the use of daylight and contributes to thermal comfort, reducing the need for artificial lighting and heating. The design should also consider the sun's angle during different seasons, incorporating overhangs or landscaping features that mitigate the intensity of the summer sun while welcoming the softer winter light, thus maintaining a balance between light intake and thermal comfort.

Light-Enhancing Interior Choices

The interior design of a barndominium can significantly amplify the presence of natural light within the space, turning it into a luminous haven. Reflective surfaces play a crucial role in this enhancement, with polished floors, glossy finishes, and mirrored accents acting as light multipliers, bouncing daylight into the nooks and crannies of rooms. The choice of a light color palette, favoring whites, creams, and pastels, further elevates this effect, creating a backdrop reflecting light and imbuing the space with airiness and openness. The selection of sheer, lightweight fabrics for window treatments ensures that, while privacy is maintained, light is not barricaded outside, allowing it to filter through and fill the room with a soft, diffused glow.

Balancing Light and Privacy

While the pursuit of natural light is a noble endeavor, it must be tempered with privacy considerations, especially in areas where the proximity to neighbors or the public eye warrants seclusion. The strategic placement of windows becomes paramount, locating them to capture light while obscuring direct lines of sight from outside. Frosted or textured glass offers a solution, permitting light entry while blurring the details of the interior, a compromise that maintains privacy without sacrificing brightness. Window treatments, too, have evolved beyond mere decoration to become instruments of privacy management. Curtains and blinds, designed for easy adjustment, allow the inhabitants to modulate visibility and light intake as needed, providing control over the interplay of illumination and seclusion. Additionally, the landscaping surrounding the barndominium can serve as a natural barrier, with trees and shrubs positioned to shield windows from view while permitting light to penetrate the foliage, harmonizing privacy with the desire for a sunlit home.

In crafting a barndominium where natural light is not just a guest but a resident, the marriage of architectural innovation, design forethought, and interior savvy becomes essential. This conflux, where light is maximized, orientation is optimized, interiors amplified, and privacy is preserved, transforms the space into a beacon of light, an embodiment of the home's connection to the natural world. Through these strategies, the barndominium becomes a canvas on which the sun paints its daily masterpiece, a testament to the power of light to shape our environments and well-being.

EXTERIOR DESIGN: MAKING A STATEMENT

The exterior of a barndominium serves as the prologue to its interior narrative, offering a glimpse into the aesthetic journey that awaits within. This initial impression, crafted with intention and an eye for detail, sets the stage for the home's identity, blending the ruggedness of its agricultural heritage with the polished finesse of modern living. Here, in the facade that greets the world, the tone of the barndominium's design story is first struck, a harmony of materials, details, and forms that beckons the viewer into a space where history and progress dance in unison.

First Impressions Matter

The significance of a barndominium's exterior cannot be overstated, for it is the silent communicator of the home's character and the dweller's ethos. A well-conceived design captivates the onlooker and imbues the structure with a sense of place and purpose. The careful orchestration of architectural lines, the thoughtful play of shadows and light, and the strategic use of materials transform the exterior from mere walls to a canvas of expression. This articulation of the home's facade, whether through the boldness of geometric forms or the subtlety of texture interplay, invites the viewer into a deeper appreciation of the craftsmanship and vision that birthed the structure.

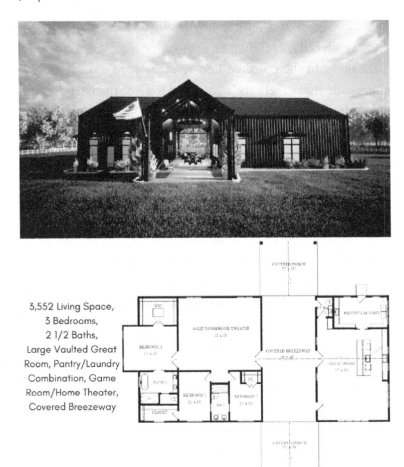

3,552 Living Space,
3 Bedrooms,
2 1/2 Baths,
Large Vaulted Great
Room, Pantry/Laundry
Combination, Game
Room/Home Theater,
Covered Breezeway

Material Choices

The palette from which the barndominium's exterior is painted draws from a well of materials that respect both durability and aesthetic appeal. With its sleek finish and resilience, metal siding offers a nod to the home's utilitarian roots while providing a modern sheath that stands defiant against the elements. Wood, aged by time or treated to endure, wraps the structure in a warmth that speaks of nature and nostalgia, a tactile link to the earth and its timeless beauty. Whether in rugged cladding or precise masonry, stone accents lend weight and solidity to the design, grounding the home in the permanence of the land upon which it sits. Together, these materials weave a facade that is a shield against time and weather and a testament to the fusion of endurance and elegance that defines the barndominium.

1,600 SqFt Living Space, 2 Bedrooms, 1 Bath, Vaulted Great Room, Covered Porch, 4 Car Garage

Landscaping Integration

Beyond the confines of the barndominium, the land it rests on plays a pivotal role in the exterior design narrative. When approached with a vision that unites the home to its environment, landscaping erases the hard lines that might separate structure from setting, fostering a seamless transition that celebrates the unity of built and natural. Native plantings that reflect the local flora, gardens that conform to the land's contours, and inviting pathways all contribute to a landscape design that serves as both a frame for and an extension of the barndominium, enhancing its connection with the environment. Water features, whether a tranquil pond that reflects the sky or a babbling brook that sings with the sound of movement, add a dynamic element to the setting, a reminder of nature's presence and the cyclical flow of life.

Custom Architectural Features

In distinguishing a barndominium from its peers, custom architectural features act as the signatures of the artist, unique flourishes that imbue the structure with personality and distinction. A porch that wraps around the building, offering vistas and shelter, becomes a place of gathering and reflection, a bridge between the interior sanctuary and the wilds beyond. With their intricate designs, decorative gables punctuate the roofline, casting patterns of shadow and light that evolve with the day. Custom ironwork, whether gracing the entrance or adorning windows, weaves a thread of craftsmanship and artistry through the design, a nod to the hands that shaped the home. These features, each carefully considered and executed, serve not only as embellishments but also as integral elements of the barndominium's identity, markers of a house that is a singular reflection of its inhabitants' tastes and aspirations.

In the realm of barndominium design, the exterior serves as prologue and promise, an initial impression that hints at the richness of the narrative within. Through the thoughtful selection of materials, the integration of the home into its landscape, and the incorporation of custom features that speak of craftsmanship and care, the barndominium's facade becomes a statement, a declaration of style, substance, and the seamless melding of past and present. In this articulation of the exterior, the barndominium finds its voice, inviting onlookers and inhabitants alike into a space where every line, texture, and detail tells a part of the more remarkable story that unfolds within its walls.

3,028 SqFt Living
Space, 3 Bedrooms,
2 1/2 Baths,
Covered Porch,
Sloped Great Room,
Loft, Outdoor Kitchen,
Outdoor Fireplace

INTERIOR DESIGN FOR BARNDOMINIUMS: A ROOM-BY-ROOM GUIDE

In the realm of barndominium living, where the essence of rustic heritage weds with the clarity of modern design, there is an opportunity to craft spaces that resonate deeply with someone's personal narrative and functional desires. This section delves into the art of tailoring each room to reflect a harmonious blend of individual style and practicality, weaving a seamless thread of cohesion through diverse themes while exploring unique room functionalities that echo the distinct lifestyle of barndominium dwellers.

Personalizing Spaces

The task of infusing each room with personal flair while addressing the needs of its occupants calls for an intimate dialogue between the dweller's lifestyle and the interior's capacity to adapt. In the bedroom, where tranquility reigns supreme, incorporating elements like a handpicked vintage headboard or custom-made quilts can infuse the space with intimacy and warmth, making it a true reflection of the occupant's taste and history. For living areas, a carefully curated collection of art or family heirlooms displayed prominently adds character and anchors the room in stories and memories, transforming it into a living gallery of personal milestones.

Room Reflection Exercise

- Select a room to focus on and list what activities typically occur there.
- Identify items of personal significance that you want to incorporate into this room.
- Imagine the ideal atmosphere of this room. What colors, textures, and materials come to mind?
- Sketch or describe how you would arrange these elements to balance functionality with personal style.

This exercise encourages thoughtful consideration of how personal items and design choices can combine to create a functional and deeply personal space.

Functional Aesthetics

Achieving a synergy of beauty and utility in each room demands an innovative approach where form meets function in an elegant dance. In the kitchen, the integration of sleek, energy-efficient appliances alongside rustic, reclaimed wood cabinetry exemplifies this balance, offering modern convenience without sacrificing the warmth and charm inherent to barndominium aesthetics. Bathrooms, often spaces of utilitarian blandness, can transform into havens of relaxation with the addition of a vintage claw-foot tub juxtaposed against the clean lines of minimalist fixtures, proving that functionality need not be devoid of elegance.

Cohesive Themes

Maintaining a unified design theme across the expansive canvas of a barndominium challenges the designer to tread carefully between variety and uniformity. This cohesion is achieved not through replicating identical design elements in every room but through the subtle threading of common themes or motifs throughout the home. It uses natural wood and stone consistently across different spaces, whether as primary materials or accent touches, and can serve as a visual and tactile thread that ties the rooms together. Similarly, a color palette that draws from the same family of hues, although in varied shades, ensures a seamless flow of space without repetition.

Design Cohesion Checklist

- Identify a core material or texture to be incorporated in each room.
- Select a base color palette that will flow through your entire home.
- Choose one or two design motifs (e.g., geometric shapes, botanical prints) to recur subtly in various spaces.
- Consider the lighting design as a unifying element across rooms.

This checklist can help ensure that while each room has its unique character, a cohesive design language is maintained throughout your barndominium.

Unique Room Ideas

The architectural flexibility of barndominiums opens up a realm of possibilities for custom room functionalities that cater to the unique hobbies and lifestyles of the occupants. An integrated workshop with robust workbenches and ample storage for tools and materials can provide a sanctuary for the artisan or artist, blending seamlessly with the living areas while offering a dedicated space for creation and innovation. For the avid reader or writer, a library or study adorned with floor-to-ceiling bookshelves and a commanding desk against expansive windows offers a tranquil retreat for contemplation and creativity.

Crafted to match the passions and interests of their residents, these spaces transform the barndominium from a simple home into a platform for personal expression. Each room is a tribute to the inhabitant's journey and dreams, going beyond mere functionality. Through this careful orchestration of design elements, the barndominium interior becomes a symphony of personal style, practicality, and unity, a harmonious abode that embraces the full spectrum of living and being.

SMART STORAGE SOLUTIONS FOR CLUTTER-FREE LIVING

In the realm of barndominium living, where the expanse of open space invites light and life to fill its broad embrace, the specter of clutter looms as a challenge to tranquility and order. Pursuing solutions that meld innovation with ingenuity becomes a quest not merely for storage but for preserving this sanctuary's grace. Within these walls, where rustic charm meets modern efficiency, the integration of intelligent storage solutions emerges as a narrative of balance, a tale of spaces that breathe freely yet hold within their embrace the myriad elements of daily existence.

Innovative Storage Ideas

Navigating the distinctive architectural terrain of a barndominium requires a storage approach that surpasses traditional limits, delving into the in-between spaces and structural intricacies as possible havens for organization. The lofty heights of vaulted ceilings beckon with the promise of vertical storage, where bespoke shelving reaches upward, transforming unused air into a gallery of possessions neatly displayed or concealed. Underfoot, the innovation continues with floorboards that lift to reveal compartments hidden beneath the surface, a secret cache for seasonal items or those infrequently used. Even the walls offer a canvas for creativity, with recessed niches carved into their breadth, providing homes for books, art, or memories in a display that marries form with function.

Multipurpose Furniture

The chemistry of transforming furniture into storage vessels is a practice that imbues the barndominium with a dynamic versatility, each piece a study in the art of diversity. Consider the humble ottoman, which, upon revelation, doubles as a repository for linens or leisure reads. Dining tables unfold to unveil compartments beneath their surfaces, offering sanctuary for cutlery or craft supplies. Beds, too, join this chorus of versatility, with frames that conceal drawers or entire compartments beneath their mattresses, a dual domain of rest and repository. This approach to furniture selection invites a reconsideration of each item's role within the home, challenging them to serve not just in their primary function but as active participants in the quest for clutter-free living.

Built-In Solutions

The architectural integrity of a barndominium lends itself to the elegance of built-in storage solutions, each integration a seamless fusion of form and utility. Cabinetry that stretches from floor to ceiling, following the line of the walls, creates a uniformity of design while offering abundant space for the concealment of household goods. Window seats are adorned with cushions, hide drawers, or are open to deep cavities beneath, yoking the joy of leisure with the practicality of storage. Even staircases, in their ascent, reveal opportunities for organization, with each step a potential drawer and the spaces beneath transformed into closets or shelving units. These built-in solutions honor the aesthetic of the barndominium while embedding within its structure the means to a clutter-free existence.

Decluttering Strategies

Culturing a clutter-free environment within the expansive embrace of a barndominium is an ongoing endeavor, a practice that intertwines discipline with design. The first step in this journey is adopting a minimalist mindset, a commitment to the presence within the home, and only those items that serve a purpose or spark joy. This philosophy of intentional living extends into the realms of organization, where every possession is assigned a home, a designated space that awaits its return after use. Regular audits of belongings, guided by the questions of necessity and delight, ensure that accumulation is curbed and that which remains is worthy of the space it occupies. Finally, tidying becomes a daily practice, a few moments at the day's beginning or end devoted to restoring order, ensuring the barndominium remains a bastion of tranquility amid the storm of life.

In this section, the exploration of intelligent storage solutions within the barndominium unfolds as a narrative of innovation, versatility, and intention. It speaks to the potential of spaces, both seen and unseen, to harbor the essentials of daily life in a manner that respects the aesthetic and spirit of the home. Through inventive approaches to storage, the multipurpose reimagining of furniture, the seamless integration of built-in solutions, and the disciplined pursuit of decluttering, the barndominium rises as a sanctuary of order and beauty, a testament to the notion that in the harmony of design and organization, there lies freedom.

CHOOSING MATERIALS: AESTHETIC, COST, AND SUSTAINABILITY CONSIDERATIONS

Selecting materials for a barndominium is akin to an alchemist's pursuit, where elements are mixed with precision, aiming for a result that transcends the sum of its parts. This intricate process involves a delicate balancing act: aligning the visual appeal with financial pragmatism and ecological responsibility. Each choice carries its weight, influencing not just the immediate ambiance but the long-term livability and impact of the home.

In navigating this complex landscape, the initial step involves a deep dive into understanding the inherent qualities of potential materials. This involves considering their source and the energy required for their production, alongside their longevity and eventual disposal or reuse. Wood, for instance, offers warmth and a direct link to nature but varies widely in its environmental footprint depending on its source and treatment. Steel, celebrated for its strength and recyclability, presents an industrial aesthetic that can be softened with thoughtful design or left raw for a more stark, modern appeal. Concrete, with its versatility and durability, offers a blank canvas for textural play and color but requires consideration for its thermal properties and impact on the interior climate.

Pursuing eco-friendly options is not merely a nod to current trends but a deeply rooted decision reflecting a commitment to sustainability. Bamboo is a renewable resource that proliferates, offering a durable yet lightweight option for flooring or decorative elements. Recycled steel, repurposed from previous uses, reduces the demand for virgin materials and the environmental cost of production. Insulation from natural fibers like wool or recycled cotton keeps the home temperate. It contributes to healthier indoor air quality and is accessible from the off-gassing associated with some synthetic insulations.

The cost-benefit analysis of these choices often reveals a narrative that extends beyond initial expenses to encompass life-cycle costs and savings. For example, the upfront cost of installing high-quality insulation or choosing triple-glazed windows might be higher. Still, the reduction in heating and cooling expenses over time paints a picture of significant long-term savings. Similarly, investing in durable materials like stone for countertops or reclaimed hardwood for floors can result in lower maintenance and replacement costs, affirming the adage that quality pays for itself.

The aesthetic impact of material choices on the barndominium cannot be understated. It is here, in the textures, colors, and finishes, that the home finds its voice. A polished concrete floor can reflect light and lend an air of spaciousness to a room, while rough-hewn stone walls can anchor a space with their solidity and texture. The interplay of matte and gloss, rough and smooth, organic and manufactured, creates a sensory experience that defines the home's character. The visual continuity or contrast between materials can delineate spaces, guide movement, and evoke emotions, turning the barndominium into a canvas where every choice contributes to the overall composition of the home.

In this elaborate dance of selecting materials, where aesthetics, cost, and sustainability converge, the barndominium is a testament to thoughtful design. It stands as a structure that not only shelters but also inspires, conserves, and endures, a reflection of the values and visions of those who call it home. Through careful consideration and deliberate choice, the materials that form its essence interlace a narrative of balance, beauty, and responsibility, crafting a space that resonates with the past, embraces the present, and looks forward to a sustainable future.

CUSTOM FEATURES THAT MAKE YOUR BARNDOMINIUM STAND OUT

In creating a barndominium, the infusion of custom features marks the distinction between a house and a home, imprinting upon it the indelible signature of its inhabitants. In these bespoke elements, a barndominium finds its voice, articulating through design the nuanced stories and unique identities of those who dwell within. The endeavor to incorporate such elements is not merely an act of personalization but a celebration of creativity, innovation, and the singular beauty of tailored craftsmanship.

Unique Design Elements

The allure of incorporating unique design elements into a barndominium lies in their capacity to transform spaces into narratives of aesthetic distinction and personal significance.

Custom metalwork, with its intricate patterns and robust presence, serves as an architectural or decorative embellishment and a testament to the artisan's skill and the homeowner's vision. From wrought iron stair railings that spiral elegantly to hand-forged door handles that greet with their uniqueness, metalwork imbues the barndominium with a tactile richness and visual depth. Similarly, the use of reclaimed materials, each piece carrying a history of its own, adds layers of texture and story to the home. A wall clad in weathered barn wood or a countertop hewn from an old bowling alley lane not only recycles the past but also integrates it into the present, allowing the barndominium to resonate with echoes of times gone by and lives lived elsewhere.

Personal Touches

Including personal touches endows a barndominium with the essence of its occupants, incorporating the threads of their lives into its core, passions, and journeys. This personal reflection might manifest in various expressions, from a gallery wall adorned with photographs that chronicle family adventures to a commissioned bookshelf cradling volumes of cherished literature. Such personal accents adorn and animate the space, imbuing each room with the spirit of those who inhabit it. The crafting of a nook dedicated to a beloved hobby or the display of artifacts gathered from travels infuses the barndominium with a palpable sense of identity and belonging, making it unmistakably reflective of its owners.

Innovative Technology

Integrating innovative technology into a barndominium elevates modern sophistication and functionality in a world where convenience and efficiency are prized. Smart home systems that allow for the seamless control of lighting, temperature, and security from a smartphone or tablet offer ease of use and contribute to the home's energy efficiency and safety. Advanced appliances that anticipate needs and adapt to usage patterns enhance the functionality of spaces like kitchens and laundry rooms, making daily tasks less of a chore and more of a pleasure. When done in a way that complements rather than dominates the design, the thoughtful incorporation of technology ensures that the barndominium remains a place of comfort, convenience, and sustainability.

Outdoor Living Spaces

Extending the barndominium's aesthetic and ethos into the outdoors creates a seamless transition between interior and exterior spaces, expanding the realm of living into the embrace of nature. Designing outdoor living spaces that reflect the home's architectural style and the inhabitants' lifestyle preferences turns these areas into vibrant extensions of the barndominium. A patio that mirrors the interior's design language, furnished for relaxation and social gatherings, obscures interior and exterior distinctions. An outdoor kitchen equipped for culinary adventures under the open sky invites the joys of dining alfresco, making meals memorable experiences. Whether manicured or wild, landscaped gardens are spaces of exploration and reflection that connect the home to the natural world in a dialogue of growth and beauty.

In integrating these custom features, the barndominium transcends its structural form to embody the dreams, stories, and identities of those who call it home. It stands as a testament to human creativity, a space where design and innovation meet personal history and vision in a celebration of unique living. Such a home is not just built; it is crafted with intention, love, and a deep respect for the singularity of its existence.

As we draw this exploration closer, it is evident that the journey of creating a barndominium is one of imagination, innovation, and intimate personal expression. Through the thoughtful incorporation of unique design elements, personal touches, innovative technology, and outdoor living spaces, each barndominium emerges as a distinctive sanctuary, reflective of its inhabitants' lives and aspirations. These custom features not only enhance the aesthetic and functional appeal of the barndominium but also anchor it in the personal narrative of its owners, making it a true home in every sense. As we venture forward, let these principles guide us in crafting spaces that resonate with individuality, embrace modernity, and celebrate the art of living well.

2,950 SqFt Living Space, 1,600 Covered Porch, 3 Bedroom, 2 Bath, Flex Space, Smuggler's Pantry/Laundry Combo, Vaulted covered Porch, Outdoor Kitchen

HELP OTHERS DISCOVER THE MAGIC OF BARNDOMINIUMS

EMPOWER DREAMS, TRANSFORM LIVES

"People who dream of owning their own home, crafting their sustainable haven, are not just dreamers; they are architects of change, builders of futures."

— M.R. BOSS

Would you be willing to extend a helping hand to someone you've never met but whose dreams resonate with your own? Picture this: someone like you, with aspirations of turning their vision into reality but lacking guidance and support.

At the heart of our mission lies the belief that everyone deserves the opportunity to embrace the lifestyle of barndominium living. Every endeavor, every word written in *Barndominiums: Maximize Design Efficiency for Open-Concept Living*, stems from this mission. And the only way to truly achieve it is by reaching out to as many individuals as possible.

This is where your generosity can make a world of difference. It's a simple ask but one that holds immense potential to impact lives. By leaving a review for this book, you're not just offering your thoughts; you're offering hope and inspiration to countless dreamers out there.

Your review can serve as a guiding light, helping aspiring homeowners, entrepreneurs, and families realize their dreams of sustainable living. It takes just a moment of your time, but the ripple effects of your kindness can last a lifetime.

To leave your review and be a part of this transformative journey, simply scan the QR code below:

[

Join us in building a community where dreams thrive, and possibilities abound. Your support is not only appreciated; it's the fuel that propels us forward in our mission to empower others.

Thank you for your generosity and belief in the power of dreams. Together, we can make a difference, one review at a time.

Warm regards,

M.R. BOSS

4

THE BUILD PROCESS

In the vast tapestry of constructing a barndominium, laying the foundation is similar to setting the opening scene of a grand play—the strength and stability of the entire structure rest upon this initial act. Much like a seasoned conductor leading an orchestra, the process demands precision, insight, and a mindful coordination of elements to ensure the harmony of the outcome. It's a phase where the raw land meets the vision, transforming through meticulous steps into a base supporting a structure and a future home filled with dreams and possibilities.

LAYING THE FOUNDATION: A STEP-BY-STEP GUIDE

Foundation Types

The choice of foundation is not to be taken lightly, as it impacts the stability and durability of a barndominium and its interaction with the surrounding environment. Slab, pier and beam, and basement foundations each have their place, dictated by the build site's geography, soil composition, and climate. For instance, slab foundations, while cost-effective and quick to install, best suit regions with stable, non-expansive soils. In contrast, areas prone to flooding or with significant soil movement might better accommodate pier and beam foundations, offering elevation and flexibility. Basements offering additional living or storage space require careful consideration of water drainage and insulation to fend off moisture and cold.

Preparation Steps

Preparing the site for foundation laying differs from preparing a canvas for painting. It begins with clearing the land of vegetation, debris, and any obstacles that could impede construction. The next phase is to grade the site, a critical step that ensures proper drainage away from the foundation, safeguarding the structure from water damage. It's a phase where precision instruments and a keen eye for detail are indispensable, ensuring the site is level and ready for the foundation forms.

Construction Process

Building the foundation is a carefully choreographed dance, with every stage, from positioning the forms to pouring the concrete, demanding exact timing and flawless execution. The process starts with installing forms and temporary molds that shape the concrete as it sets. For a slab foundation, a layer of gravel is first spread to facilitate drainage, followed by installing a moisture barrier. Reinforcing steel bars (rebar) are placed to strengthen the concrete, a critical step to prevent cracking under the weight of the barndominium. Concrete pouring is meticulous, requiring a steady hand and a watchful eye to ensure it fills every corner of the form and around the rebar, eliminating air pockets that could weaken the structure. Once poured, the concrete must cure, a process that might take days or weeks, depending on the size and complexity of the foundation.

Common Challenges

Challenges can arise during the foundation-laying process, even with the best-laid plans. Unforeseen soil conditions, such as unexpected rock formations or water tables, can necessitate a pivot in foundation type or additional preparatory work. Weather plays a fickle role, with rain or extreme temperatures potentially delaying pours or affecting curing times. Navigating these hurdles requires flexibility, an experienced construction team, and, sometimes, a dash of creativity. For example, when faced with a sudden rain forecast before a pour, quickly covering the site with tarps can save the day, preventing the groundwork from being washed away.

Foundation Checklist

To guide you through this critical phase, here's a checklist to ensure all bases are covered:

1. Assess soil type and environmental conditions to choose the appropriate foundation type.

2. Clear and grade the site, ensuring proper drainage and a level base.
3. Install forms for the foundation, paying close attention to dimensions and alignments.
4. Spread gravel and install a moisture barrier for slab foundations.
5. Lay rebar within the forms for added strength.
6. Schedule the concrete pour, monitoring weather conditions closely.
7. Allow the concrete to cure fully before proceeding with construction.

This checklist serves as a roadmap, ensuring that each step in laying the foundation is performed with the attention to detail it deserves, setting the stage for the rest of the construction process to unfold smoothly.

FRAMING AND STRUCTURAL ELEMENTS OF BARNDOMINIUMS

Framing Basics

In the architectural anatomy of a barndominium, the skeleton—comprised of meticulously assembled beams, posts, and trusses—dictates not merely the edifice's stature but its very soul. This skeletal framework, known as framing, serves as the backbone, supporting walls, roofs, and floors while shaping the interior's three-dimensional configuration. Traditionally, wood has been the preferred choice for its natural resilience and ease of manipulation. However, the advent of steel framing has introduced a new paradigm, offering unmatched durability and resistance to elements, pests, and fire. The framing technique involves precise measurements and cutting of these materials and their assembly into a coherent structure. Each piece interlocks within this framework, orchestrated through a series of standardized practices and innovative methods, ensuring the envisioned form of the barndominium comes to life with structural integrity and aesthetic fidelity.

Structural Integrity

The assurance of structural integrity in a barndominium transcends the mere adherence to building codes; it is a pledge of safety, longevity, and resilience. The meticulous design process begins, where architects and engineers collaborate, considering load distribution, wind resistance, and seismic activity. The employment of advanced software models simulates stress and strain on the structure, guiding the optimization of framing layouts to distribute weight evenly and ensure stability. Critical to this endeavor is the quality of materials selected, where higher-grade lumber or steel, treated for environmental resistance, forms the brawn and bones of the building. The anchoring of the frame to the foundation with precision-engineered fasteners and connectors further solidifies this integrity, creating a unified structure that stands defiant against the forces of nature.

Innovative Framing Solutions

The evolution of framing practices has ushered in a realm where functionality melds with aesthetic ambition, birthing innovative solutions that elevate both. One such innovation, prefabricated panels and trusses, streamlines the construction process. These elements, crafted off-site to exact specifications and then transported to the building site, not only accelerate the erection of the frame but also minimize waste and labor costs. Another avant-garde approach is the integration of hybrid framing, where wood and steel fuse within a single structure. This method harnesses the aesthetic warmth of wood and the structural prowess of steel, yielding a visually appealing and exceptionally sturdy frame. Further, incorporating green framing techniques emphasizes sustainability, utilizing materials from renewable sources and designs that minimize thermal bridging, enhancing the energy efficiency of the barndominium.

Inspection and Compliance

Navigating the labyrinth of local building codes and regulations is a critical phase in the framing process, ensuring that the structure stands firm and does so within the legal framework. The inspection of the frame, conducted by certified professionals, scrutinizes every joint, beam, and connection, comparing them against stringent standards. This scrutiny ensures that the structural elements are correctly installed, with suitable materials and methods, safeguarding the integrity of the building. Compliance extends beyond the mere structural to encompass environmental considerations, with inspectors assessing the frame's alignment with energy efficiency and sustainability standards. This rigorous process, while demanding, acts as a guardian of quality, ensuring that the barndominium not only provides a haven for its inhabitants but also contributes positively to the architectural tapestry of the community.

In the grand orchestra of constructing a barndominium, the framing stage is a symphony of strength, precision, and innovation. The vision takes physical form here, rising from the foundation to sketch a home's silhouette. Through the basics of framing, a commitment to structural integrity, the exploration of innovative solutions, and the diligent pursuit of inspection and compliance, the barndominium evolves. It becomes a structure and testament to the harmony of resilience and design. It promises a sanctuary that will endure through generations, weathering the changes of time and nature with grace.

ELECTRICAL AND PLUMBING ESSENTIALS FOR YOUR BARNDOMINIUM

The electrical and plumbing systems, the veins and arteries of any home, demand a meticulous approach from inception through realization. They ensure the functionality and efficiency of a barndominium and its safety and adaptability to future innovations. This segment navigates the intricacies of planning, implementing, and refining these critical systems, emphasizing the equilibrium between energy conservation, operational safety, and the discerning choice between professional engagement and personal undertaking in installations.

Planning and Layout

The initiation of electrical and plumbing frameworks hinges on a forward-thinking layout, meticulously orchestrated to align with architectural blueprints yet flexible enough to adapt to evolving technologies and living habits. With its circuitry planned to minimize distance and optimize load distribution, the electrical layout must account for current needs while anticipating future expansions or technological upgrades, such as smart home integrations. Conversely, plumbing requires an unyielding focus on the gravitational pull for waste removal, paired with an efficient supply system that ensures water is delivered where needed without compromise. This phase benefits from collaborative input, involving architects, electricians, and plumbers to overlay their expertise. This combined knowledge ensures that outlets, fixtures, and pipes enhance rather than deter from the living experience, integrated seamlessly into walls, floors, and ceilings.

Energy Efficiency

In an era where sustainability is not just valued but vital, designing electrical and plumbing systems with an emphasis on energy efficiency is paramount. For electricity, this involves strategically placing fixtures and outlets to maximize natural light, reducing reliance on artificial sources during daylight hours. LED lighting has become the default with its lower energy consumption and longer life-span. At the same time, advanced HVAC systems are selected for their ability to conserve energy without sacrificing comfort. Plumbing systems, meanwhile, embrace low-flow fixtures and on-demand water heaters, significantly reducing water usage and the energy required to heat it. Incorporating greywater systems for non-potable uses further exemplifies the commitment to minimizing environmental impact and reusing water for landscaping or flushing toilets.

Safety Considerations

The paramountcy of safety in electrical and plumbing installations cannot be overstated, with strict adherence to codes and standards acting as the guardian of household well-being. Electrical systems, with their potential fire or electrocution hazard, necessitate rigorous inspections, ensuring that wiring, outlets, and panels meet or exceed safety requirements. Ground Fault Circuit Interrupters (GFCIs) become a staple in areas prone to moisture, offering added protection against electrical shock. Plumbing, while less overtly hazardous, carries risks from leaks leading to mold and structural damage to the proper venting of gases to prevent buildup. Here, the selection of materials and the precision of installation play critical roles, with pipes and fixtures needing to withstand uncompromising pressures and temperatures.

Professional vs. DIY

The delineation between tasks suited for professional hands and those within the realm of DIY enthusiasts is not merely a question of skill but of understanding each system's complexity and potential impact. Given its inherent risks and the intricacies of local codes, electrical work often necessitates professional involvement, ensuring the installation is safe, efficient, and compliant. Plumbing, while seemingly more approachable for the experienced DIYer, still requires a profound understanding of system design and local regulations, particularly for main lines or waste removal. Smaller projects, such as fixture replacements or minor repairs, may fall comfortably within the DIY domain, offering a sense of accomplishment and personal involvement in the home's evolution. However, the line is drawn where safety and complexity dictate, urging deference to professionals who carry not just the tools but the knowledge essential for such critical components of home construction.

In navigating the electrical and plumbing landscapes of a barndominium, one becomes acutely aware of the balance between form and function, innovation and tradition, and personal endeavor with professional expertise. These systems, while often concealed behind walls or beneath floors, are the lifeblood of the home, demanding respect, foresight, and an unwavering commitment to quality and safety. Through careful planning, a focus on energy efficiency, adherence to safety protocols, and a discerning approach to the division of labor, the barndominium rises not just as a structure but as a testament to thoughtful design and sustainable living, ready to adapt and flourish in the face of tomorrow's challenges.

INSULATION AND ENERGY EFFICIENCY BEST PRACTICES

Choosing Insulation

Selecting the suitable insulation material for a barndominium is a decision embedded into the fabric of sustainability, comfort, and cost-effectiveness. With its widespread availability and cost-efficiency, fiberglass presents a popular choice, yet its performance must be balanced against environmental considerations and potential health risks during installation. Cellulose, crafted from recycled paper and treated for fire resistance, emerges as an eco-friendly alternative, embodying high R-values—the measure of thermal resistance—and sound-dampening qualities. Meanwhile, spray foam insulation, though pricier, offers unparalleled air sealing capabilities, molding itself into every nook, cranny, and crevice to form a monolithic barrier against heat transfer. In regions burdened by extreme temperatures, rigid foam boards or reflective insulation may supplement these choices, tailored to specific needs, whether augmenting underfoot warmth in a chill-prone living space or deflecting the sun's relentless gaze in sun-drenched locales. The selection process, steeped in an understanding of R-values and the unique demands of the barndominium's geography, becomes a calculated endeavor to link efficiency with environmental stewardship.

Installation Techniques

Installing insulation transcends mere placement; it is an exercise in precision, ensuring that the protective layer envelops the barndominium in a continuous thermal blanket. For batt and roll insulation, such as fiberglass, the key lies in cutting the material to fit snugly between joists and studs, avoiding compression or gaps that would diminish its effectiveness. Spray foam, applied as a liquid, expands to fill cavities, demanding a skilled hand to achieve an even distribution without overexpansion. The technique of layering, especially in attics or basements, where temperatures fluctuate most, involves applying successive layers of insulation, each contributing to a cumulative R-value that shields the interior from external whims. In this meticulous process, sealing air-leaks around windows, doors, and fixtures with caulk or weather-stripping becomes equally pivotal, addressing the invisible thieves of heat and cool.

Additional Energy Efficiency Measures

Beyond the bulwark of insulation, additional measures beckon, each a step toward a more sustainable, energy-conservative barndominium. Installing energy-efficient windows with double or triple panes, low-emissivity coatings, and inert gas fills is a testament to this commitment, reducing heat transfer and UV exposure. Similarly, the choice of insulated and weather-stripped exterior doors fortifies the home against the elements, ensuring that the comfort within remains undisturbed by the whims of weather. Adopting LED lighting, programmable thermostats, and ENERGY STAR-rated appliances further this endeavor, each reduction in electricity or gas consumption a victory for both the homeowner and the planet. In spaces where the sun's bounty is plentiful, integrating solar panels offsets energy costs and contributes surplus power back to the grid, embodying the pinnacle of energy efficiency and sustainability.

Long-Term Benefits

The prioritization of insulation and energy efficiency in constructing a barndominium unfolds a tapestry of long-term benefits, each a testament to foresight and investment in the future. The immediate comfort experienced through consistent indoor temperatures, free from the drafts and cold spots that mar lesser-insulated homes, is but the first of these rewards. Financial incentives manifest in reduced utility bills, the savings accruing over months and years, often offsetting the initial outlay for premium insulation or energy-efficient fixtures. Though less tangible, the environmental impact is no less significant, with decreased energy consumption translating to lower carbon emissions, contributing to the global effort to stem the tide of climate change. Furthermore, the enhanced durability and moisture control afforded by effective insulation and sealing techniques protects the structural integrity of the barndominium, warding off the decay and damage wrought by uncontrolled humidity or pest infiltration. In this light, the barndominium stands not just as a structure but as a beacon of sustainable living, its walls a shield against the elements, its systems a model of efficiency, and its presence a testament to the harmonious balance between human habitation and environmental protection.

ROOFING OPTIONS: DURABILITY AND DESIGN

The selection of roofing material for a barndominium is an endeavor that transcends mere coverage; it is a subtle decision that intertwines durability with aesthetics, marrying the practical with the visually appealing, all while keeping a keen eye on budgetary considerations. Various materials beckon, each with its attributes and drawbacks, ranging from traditional asphalt shingles, known for their cost-effectiveness and ease of installation, to metal roofing, which offers unmatched longevity and resistance to the elements. Then there are the more unconventional choices like clay tiles, which, while heavier and more expensive, imbue a property with timeless elegance and can withstand decades of exposure with minimal maintenance. Similarly, slate, the embodiment of durability, carries a hefty price tag but compensates with a lifespan that can eclipse a century, along with a natural beauty that is both stately and subdued.

The architectural DNA of a barndominium, with its blend of rustic charm and modern simplicity, demands a roofing design that complements its unique aesthetic while fulfilling functional roles. The pitch and slope, for instance, do more than dictate the roof's visual profile; they influence its ability to dispel water and snow, minimizing the likelihood of leaks or structural damage. A steeper pitch, while requiring more material and thus increasing costs, offers a dramatic silhouette and superior drainage, making it a worthy consideration in regions prone to heavy precipitation. Conversely, a gently sloping or flat roof might align better with a minimalist aesthetic. It can provide additional outdoor living space or a platform for solar panels, although more attention is needed for waterproofing and drainage.

Maintaining the roof of a barndominium is critical to ensuring its longevity and preserving the home's overall integrity. Regular inspections, ideally bi-annually, allow for the early detection of potential issues, such as cracked tiles or rusting metal, that could escalate into more significant problems. Cleaning gutters and downspouts to prevent blockages, removing debris like fallen leaves or branches from the roof's surface, and checking for signs of wear around vents, chimneys, and skylights are all simple yet effective practices. For wood shingles or clay tiles, which may be more susceptible to algae or moss growth, gentle cleaning with appropriate solutions can prevent damage and maintain the roof's aesthetic appeal. Prompt repairs, whether replacing individual shingles or reapplying sealant, can fore-stall the need for more extensive, costly interventions.

Green roofs and solar tiles emerge as compelling options for innovative roofing solutions that align with the ethos of customization and sustainability inherent to barndominium living. Green roofs, with their layer of vegetation, offer a visual connection to nature, enhance insulation, reduce runoff, and improve air quality, making them an investment in both environmental and personal well-being. Solar tiles, though still evolving in terms of cost-efficiency, represent the pinnacle of integrating renewable energy solutions into home design. These photovoltaic cells, designed to mimic traditional roofing materials, harness the sun's power directly atop the home, blending aesthetic coherence with the practicality of on-site electricity generation. Both options reflect a forward-thinking approach to roofing, one that values innovation and respects the environment, embodying the spirit of the barndominium as a home that is as conscious of its footprint as it is of its form.

WINDOWS AND DOORS: SECURITY MEETS DESIGN

In a barndominium, where functionality and aesthetics are crucial, choosing the right windows and doors is essential to balance security and design. This section explores the selection criteria, installation practices, innovative options, and maintenance guidelines necessary for integrating these elements seamlessly into your living space.

Selection Criteria

Selecting the appropriate windows and doors for a barndominium involves multiple factors that contribute to the overall efficiency and safety of the home. Energy efficiency is paramount, with choices often influenced by the thermal performance of window and door materials. Double or triple-glazed units filled with inert gases like argon can significantly reduce energy costs and improve comfort. Security features are equally important, with reinforced glass and multi-point locking systems providing heightened protection against break-ins. Finally, design compatibility must be considered to ensure these elements complement the barndominium's rustic yet modern aesthetic. Choices in frame materials, such as natural wood or sleek aluminum, and finishes can enhance the visual appeal while maintaining coherence with the architectural style.

Installation Best Practices

Proper installation of windows and doors is critical to their performance and longevity. Precise measurements must be taken before ordering or customizing the units to ensure an appropriate fit. This prevents gaps that could lead to drafts or water ingress. During installation, using quality flashing and weather-resistant sealants is crucial for protecting against weather elements. Additionally, ensuring that windows and doors are level and properly aligned prevents operational difficulties, such as sticking or uneven wear. Employing a professional installer who adheres to the local building codes and manufacturer's guidelines can help achieve optimal results.

Innovative Options

Innovations in window and door technologies offer home-owners a chance to enhance their barndominium's energy efficiency and security while boosting aesthetic appeal. Energy-efficient glazing technologies, including low-E coatings, reduce UV and infrared light transmission without compromising natural light. Smart locks and access controls provide convenience and improved security, allowing smartphone remote management. For design, manufacturers now offer expansive glass panels that enhance natural lighting and visually open up spaces, blending indoor and outdoor environments seamlessly. These innovative features can be tailored to reflect the unique character of a barndominium, reinforcing its design ethos.

Maintenance and Upkeep

Maintaining the functionality and appearance of windows and doors is vital for longevity. Regular cleaning of frames and glass prevents the buildup of dirt and debris that can degrade materials and obscure visibility. Checking seals and weather-stripping annually for signs of wear and replacing them as necessary helps maintain energy efficiency. Additionally, hardware components such as hinges, locks, and handles should be inspected and lubricated regularly to ensure smooth operation. For wood frames, periodic re-staining or repainting is necessary to protect against the elements and prevent warping or rotting.

By meticulously selecting, installing, and maintaining windows and doors, homeowners can ensure these elements contribute positively to the barndominium's comfort, security, and aesthetic appeal, embodying a perfect blend of security and design.

INTERIOR FINISHING TOUCHES: FLOORING, WALLS, AND CEILINGS

In the sanctuary of a barndominium, where every corner whispers tales of innovation and dreams made tangible, the selection of flooring stands as a testament to the homeowner's character and resilience. The myriad options available, each with a unique voice and texture, invite a decision that balances the pragmatic with the poetic. Hardwood, revered for its timeless elegance and warmth, offers a canvas that ages gracefully, acquiring a patina that speaks of footsteps and stories over time. Yet, its susceptibility to moisture and wear necessitates a vigilant care regime, making it a choice for those willing to embrace its evolving beauty. Concrete, conversely, presents an ode to modernity and simplicity, its excellent, sleek surface a foundation for minimalist aesthetics. Treated with stains or textures, it transcends its industrial origins, becoming a versatile and durable stage for life's daily ballet. For spaces where comfort underfoot is paramount, luxury vinyl tile (LVT) emerges as a champion, mimicking the allure of wood or stone while offering unparalleled resistance to the scuffs and spills of domestic life.

Transitioning to the realm of walls, where vertical spaces become the canvas for personal expression, the impact of finishes on the barndominium's ambiance is profound. Paint, in its infinite spectrum of hues, offers the simplest yet most transformative tool for mood and space definition. A soft, muted palette can expand and brighten, lending airiness to compact spaces, while bold, vibrant colors command attention, portraying areas with purpose and energy. Beyond paint, applying textures such as exposed brick or shiplap adds layers of historical or rustic charm, imbuing rooms with a narrative depth that paint alone cannot achieve. Wallpaper, reborn in contemporary patterns and eco-friendly materials, offers another dimension of customization, enabling walls to don intricate designs or scenes that captivate and inspire.

Elevating our gaze to the ceilings, often the overlooked fifth wall, reveals an expanse ripe for architectural innovation. Traditional flat ceilings, while ever-present, take advantage of an opportunity to elevate the barndominium's design ethos. Vaulted or cathedral ceilings break this mold, drawing eyes upward and creating a sense of grandeur and spaciousness that mirrors the open spirit of barndominium living. For those intrigued by texture and pattern, coffered or tray ceilings provide a structured elegance, adding layers of visual interest without encroaching on the living space below. The incorporation of skylights or clerestory windows in these elevated designs enhances the architectural interest and invites natural light to play across the surfaces, changing with the time of day and season, adding a dynamic element to the static.

The narrative of a barndominium's interior culminates in the final touches that tie each element together, where trim and paint act as finishes and punctuation marks that define and refine. Baseboards and crown molding, selected with a mindful eye to scale and style, frame rooms with a subtle grace, accentuating heights and delineating boundaries. The choice of paint finish, from matte to high gloss, interacts with light and texture to create effects that range from understated elegance to dramatic flair. Door and window trim, when thoughtfully chosen, complements the architectural style, lending a cohesive look that bridges the diverse materials and colors employed throughout the home. Though seemingly minor in the grand scheme, these elements are critical in crafting a complete space where every detail is harmonious and the vision of a home that is both a refuge and a statement is fully realized.

EXTERNAL LANDSCAPING AND OUTDOOR SPACES

Integrating with the Landscape

The alignment of a barndominium within its natural surroundings does not happen by chance but through a deliberate and thoughtful process that conjoins the architectural footprint with the land's inherent character. This symbiosis begins with an acute observation of the landscape's topography, the native flora, and the directional play of sunlight across the terrain. Adapting the barndominium's orientation to embrace these elements, whether positioning living areas to capture the morning light or designing outdoor spaces that flow seamlessly into the wild, underscores respect for the land. Utilizing indigenous plants in garden areas grounds the home within its ecosystem and ensures a lower maintenance footprint, as these species have adapted to the local climate. Using natural materials, such as stone or wood, for paths and borders further blurs the lines between constructed and natural, allowing the barndo-minium to settle gracefully into its setting.

Outdoor Living Areas

Creating outdoor living spaces is an extension of the home's interior, a bridge to the world beyond its walls, offering a sanctuary where the air is fresh and the sky stretches wide. Patios become stages for family gatherings and quiet moments. Crafted from local stone or reclaimed wood, these materials echo the landscape's palette. Outdoor kitchens with grills and prep spaces invite the season's flavors into every meal, turning dining into an alfresco adventure. Adding fire pits or outdoor fireplaces, around which chairs draw close, fosters a sense of community and warmth, even as the evening chill descends. These areas, designed with shelter and openness in mind, accommodate the changing seasons, offering shade and breezes in summer, as well as warmth and protection when the weather turns. The thoughtful placement of such spaces, in harmony with the barndominium's design and the land's contours, ensures they are not just additions but integral components of living well.

2,300 SqFt Living Space, 4 Bedrooms, 2 Baths, Vaulted
Great Room, Side Porchw/ Outdoor Fireplace, Covered
Side Porch w/ Outdoor Kitchen

Landscaping for Privacy and Beauty

The dual goals of privacy and aesthetic appeal in landscaping
are achieved not through barriers but through the strategic
use of plantings and natural features. Hedges and living
walls, composed of evergreens or dense shrubs, offer seclusion while contributing texture and color to the garden's

tapestry. Incorporating water features, such as ponds or fountains, adds a layer of tranquility, their sound masking conversations and creating a private auditory space. Flower beds and ornamental trees, strategically placed, dazzle the senses with their blooms and foliage and draw the eye, directing attention away from more private areas. The use of trellises or pergolas adorned with climbing vines creates secluded nooks within the garden, intimate spaces enveloped in green. This approach to landscaping, where beauty serves as a veil for privacy, ensures that the barndominium's outdoor areas are both a feast for the senses and a retreat from the world.

Sustainable Landscaping Practices

The sustainability ethos permeates every aspect of a barndominium's existence, extending its principles into landscaping. The practice of xeriscaping aligns with this philosophy, reducing the environmental impact and maintenance demands. Rain gardens, designed to capture runoff and replenish the aquifer, function as beautiful features and stewards of the water cycle. Selecting permeable materials for paths and patios ensures that rainwater feeds the soil rather than contributing to runoff, a small act with significant implications for erosion control and water conservation. Composting organic waste to enrich the garden naturally closes the loop of sustainability, turning leftovers into life. This conscientious approach to landscaping, where every decision is weighed for its environmental impact, reflects a commitment to a lifestyle that honors the land and seeks to leave it enriched, not depleted, for generations to come.

Example of Rainwater Harvesting for Irrigation and Other Outdoor Purposes

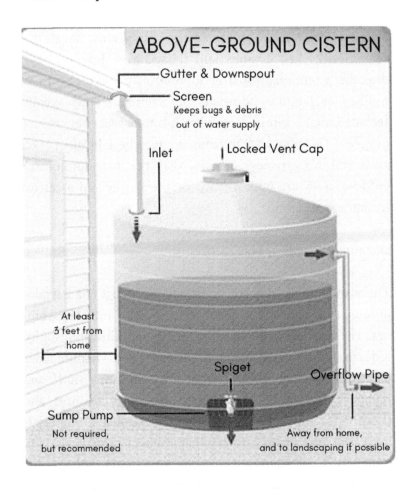

FINAL INSPECTION AND MOVE-IN CHECKLIST

Preparing for Inspection

The moment draws near when the tapestry of construction activities weaves into its final form—a barndominium ready to be scrutinized under the discerning eye of a final inspection. This phase is not merely a procedural hurdle but a critical validation of the structure's readiness, ensuring every facet aligns with safety standards and building regulations. Preparation for this inspection parallels fine-tuning an instrument before a grand performance, where attention to detail can significantly influence the outcome. Key areas typically under scrutiny include electrical systems, plumbing, structural integrity, and compliance with energy efficiency standards. Ensuring these are installed and meticulously checked for adherence to specifications can preempt potential setbacks. Conducting a pre-inspection walkthrough, armed with a checklist, is advisable to identify and rectify any issues, such as leaks, faulty wiring, or incomplete finishes, that could delay approval.

Addressing Issues

Invariably, the inspection may unveil shortcomings that require attention. This moment, while disheartening, is an opportunity for refinement. Addressing these issues promptly and precisely expedites the move-in process and reinforces the barndominium's integrity. Engaging with experienced professionals to correct identified flaws ensures that solutions are not merely superficial but address the root cause, whether in wiring anomalies, plumbing discrepancies, or insulation gaps. A detailed record of these corrections, supplemented by receipts and warranties, provides a transparent trail that facilitates re-inspection and is a valuable reference for future maintenance or resale.

Move-In Checklist

Transitioning to a barndominium from the chaos of construction to the calm of habitation is an orchestrated shift that benefits immensely from a well-conceived move-in checklist. This list serves as a bridge, guiding the final steps to ensure the space is habitable and welcoming. Essential utilities such as water, electricity, and gas must be operational, with services transferred to the new owner's name. A thorough cleaning, post-construction, purges dust and debris, setting a fresh stage for occupancy. Safety equipment should be installed and tested, including smoke detectors, carbon monoxide detectors, and fire extinguishers. An inventory of manuals and warranties for appliances and systems within the barndominium provides operation and maintenance resources. Finally, securing a home insurance policy offers protection and peace of mind as you transition into this new chapter.

Celebrating Your New Home

With the barndominium standing ready, a reflection of aspiration realized through persistence and creativity, the moment to celebrate its completion is both a culmination and a commencement. This celebration acknowledges the journey, the challenges, and the collective effort that transformed vision into reality. It invites friends and family to share in the joy and warmth of a space that will host memories, laughter, and growth. Yet, it also marks the beginning of a new phase, living and evolving within the barndominium, where every corner tells a story, and every space holds potential. In this light, the transition to residing within these walls is not merely a change of address but an embrace of a lifestyle that values uniqueness, sustainability, and the beauty of crafting a space that resonates with one's essence.

This chapter closes with the barndominium now standing as a testament to creativity, resilience, and the pursuit of sustainable living. The journey from conception to completion, fraught with challenges yet rich with rewards, mirrors the broader quest for a life that balances innovation with tradition and efficiency with aesthetics. As we step into the subsequent chapters, the focus shifts to inhabiting this space, transforming it from a structure to a home infused with personal touches, memories in the making, and the continuous evolution that defines a home that is truly alive.

2,164 SqFt Living Space, 2 Bedrooms, 2 Baths, Office & Smugglers Pantry, Outdoor Fireplace, Screened-In Side Porch, Vaulted Front Porch w/Glass Garage Door

5

FINANCING YOUR DREAM BARNDOMINIUM

Securing financing can often seem like a significant hurdle when building a home. It requires finding the right approach to transform your dream into a reality. The process of funding a barndominium combines traditional and innovative methods, each with its own set of rules and benefits. To succeed in this endeavor, you need to have a clear understanding of the various options available, a well-defined project vision, and a strategy that aligns your financial capabilities with your construction goals.

UNDERSTANDING BARNDOMINIUM FINANCING OPTIONS

Traditional Mortgages vs. Construction Loans

The choice between a traditional mortgage and a construction loan is like selecting the right tool for a specific task, where the nature of the project dictates the most fitting financial instrument. Traditional mortgages, familiar to many, offer stability with fixed rates and long-term repayments, making them suitable for properties that don't require significant alterations. However, barndominiums, often born from the ground up or through substantial renovations, frequently necessitate a more flexible funding model.

Construction loans shine in these scenarios, offering short-term financing that covers the cost of building or significant renovations. Unlike traditional mortgages paid out in a single lump sum, construction loans disburse funds in stages aligned with project milestones. This phased approach provides a financial flow that matches the construction timeline, albeit often at higher interest rates, with the expectation of converting the loan to a standard mortgage upon project completion.

For those at the crossroads of these options, the decision hinges on the project's scale and the borrower's financial readiness. A construction-to-permanent loan combines the flexibility of construction financing with the stability of a traditional mortgage, transitioning from one to the other without necessitating a second application process.

Alternative Financing

Beyond the conventional lies a spectrum of alternative financing options, each a potential key to unlocking barndominium dreams for those finding traditional routes less accessible. Unsecured personal loans, based on creditworthiness, offer a quick solution, although usually at higher interest rates and shorter repayment periods. For projects infused with innovation or community appeal, crowdfunding emerges as a viable path, tapping into the collective support of a broader audience to fund development in exchange for rewards or recognition.

Tapping into retirement savings, while a drastic measure, presents another avenue for funding. Programs like the 401(k) loan allow individuals to borrow against their retirement funds, offering a self-repaying mechanism, though with risks to future financial stability.

Navigating these alternative waters requires carefully assessing the long-term implications and costs, balancing the urgency of construction needs with the overarching goal of financial health.

Lender Requirements

Understanding the landscape from the lender's perspective illuminates the path to securing financing. Lenders seek certainty in the viability of the project and the borrower's ability to repay the loan. This certainty is often founded on detailed plans and a solid builder contract, serving as blueprints that outline the project's scope, timeline, and cost. A strong credit score, proof of income, and a sizable down payment further bolster a borrower's application, acting as financial responsibility and readiness indicators.

Preparation, then, becomes a pivotal strategy for those seeking financing. Assembling a comprehensive project dossier, complete with architectural designs, contractor bids, and a detailed budget, positions borrowers as credible and serious applicants, ready to bring their barndominium vision to life.

Case Studies of Financing Success

Real-life examples serve as beacons for navigating the complexities of financing a barndominium. Consider a couple who leveraged a construction-to-permanent loan to build their dream home on a family-owned plot of land. With detailed plans and a competitive bid from a reputable builder, they secured financing that both covered the construction phase and transitioned into a mortgage under the umbrella of a fixed interest rate that safeguarded their financial future.

Another scenario found a young entrepreneur turning to crowdfunding to finance a barndominium that doubled as a workshop and living space. By sharing the vision of a sustainable, multi-use property, the project attracted small investments from a broad audience, collectively funding the build while fostering a community of supporters invested in the project's success.

These case studies underscore the diversity of paths available, highlighting the importance of aligning financial strategies with personal circumstances and project specifics. They remind us that while the gateway of financing may seem daunting, the keys to unlocking it exist in various forms, waiting to be discovered by those who approach with diligence, creativity, and a clear vision of their dream barndominium.

Financing Checklist

To navigate barndominium financing with confidence, consider the following checklist:

- Assess your financial readiness, including credit score, income, and savings.
- Define the scope of your barndominium project, including construction or renovation needs.
- Gather detailed plans and a solid builder contract to present to lenders.
- Research and compare traditional mortgages, construction loans, and alternative financing options.
- Prepare a comprehensive project dossier for lender review.
- Consider the long-term implications of your financing choice on your financial health.
- Explore case studies and real-life examples for insights and strategies.

While not exhaustive, this checklist provides a foundational strategy for approaching barndominium financing, equipping dreamers with the tools needed to turn their vision into a reality.

BUDGETING FOR THE UNEXPECTED: CONTINGENCY PLANNING

Importance of a Contingency Fund

In the financial tapestry of constructing a barndominium, the warp and weft of expected expenses intertwine with the unpredictable threads of unforeseen costs. Within this complex weave, the necessity for a contingency fund becomes glaringly apparent, acting as a financial buffer against the unforeseen. The essence of such a fund lies not in its ability to prevent the unexpected but in its capacity to absorb the impact, ensuring that the project's momentum remains unhampered. This financial safeguard is integral to the construction budget, providing peace of mind that should the winds of fate blow unfavorably, the sails of your project will not be torn asunder.

Calculating the Right Amount

Forming an adequate contingency fund is a delicate balance between prudence and optimism. The conventional wisdom suggests allocating a percentage of the overall project budget to this fund, typically ranging between 10 and 20 percent, depending on the project's complexity and the known unknowns accompanying it. For a barndominium rising from raw earth, the higher end of this spectrum acknowledges the myriad uncertainties of groundwork and construction. Conversely, a renovation might lean toward the lower back, although with an understanding of the structure's inherent unpredictabilities. While rooted in industry standards, this calculation benefits from a tailored approach, considering factors such as the reliability of cost estimates, the project's duration, and the volatility of material prices.

Managing Contingency Funds

The stewardship of contingency funds demands discipline and a discerning eye that differentiates between necessity and extravagance. The initiation of this fund's use is not to be taken lightly, but it should be reserved for moments when alternatives have been exhausted and the unforeseen becomes unavoidable. Here, meticulous record-keeping becomes invaluable, tracking expenditures against the contingency to ensure transparency and accountability. Moreover, replenishing these funds, when circumstances allow, is crucial. Should an anticipated complication not materialize, redirecting unused portions back into the contingency ensures that it remains hearty, ready to mitigate future surprises. In essence, managing these funds is an exercise in foresight and restraint, ensuring they serve their purpose without becoming a catch-all for every overage.

Real-World Scenarios

The construction landscape is riddled with instances where contingency funds prove their worth, turning potential crises into manageable situations. Consider the discovery of rock during excavation, a not uncommon occurrence that necessitates additional machinery and labor to remove. Here, the contingency fund provides the financial agility to address the issue promptly, preventing costly delays. Similarly, the sudden unavailability of a chosen material might force a shift to a more expensive alternative. The contingency absorbs this cost difference, ensuring the project's aesthetic or functional integrity is not compromised.

Another scenario might involve regulatory changes requiring additional compliance measures post-budget approval. These funds allow for adaptation without the need for project scope reduction. Last, weather-related delays, particularly in regions prone to unexpected meteorological shifts, can extend project timelines, increasing labor and rental costs. In this case, the contingency fund acts as a financial shock absorber, ensuring these overruns do not derail the overall budget.

In these scenarios, the value of a well-considered contingency fund becomes self-evident, transforming it from a mere budgetary line item into a pivotal tool for risk management. This fund enables project continuity in the face of adversity, ensuring that the path from vision to reality remains navigable, even when beset by the unforeseen.

COST-SAVING STRATEGIES WITHOUT SACRIFICING QUALITY

Material Choices

In the nuanced tapestry of constructing a barndominium, the selection of materials is a pivotal chapter, where the narrative of cost-efficiency intertwines with the unyielding threads of quality and aesthetics. Here, the discerning eye might find that reclaimed wood tells a story of resilience and beauty and offers a testament to cost-effectiveness, unifying the rustic allure with fiscal prudence. Similarly, choosing composite materials for decking or siding represents durability and minimal maintenance, sidestepping the perennial upkeep costs associated with their natural counterparts. This arena of material selection becomes a dance of balance, a place where innovative products like luxury vinyl tile mimic the opulence of hardwood or stone yet stand in defiance of wear and the passage of time, all while keeping the budget in check. It is within this careful curation of materials that the architect—amateur or seasoned—wields the power to sculpt a space and a sanctuary that defies economic constraints without compromise.

Efficient Design

The blueprint of a barndominium serves not just as a guide for construction but as a manifesto of efficient living, where each square foot is imbued with purpose, eliminating the superfluous in favor of the essential. In this realm, the concept of multifunctional spaces emerges as a champion, where rooms adapt and transform to meet the fluid needs of daily life. A dining area by day unfurls into a cozy nook for the night's repose, challenging the conventional need for expansive, underutilized spaces. The strategic placement of windows and skylights harnesses the daily march of the sun, bathing the interiors in natural light and reducing the reliance on artificial sources. This approach to design—a tapestry woven with threads of innovation and intention—promises not only a reduction in construction costs but also heralds a future where utility bills bow to the wisdom of foresight.

Phased Building Approach

The construction of a barndominium, envisioned as a symphony of hammer and nail, might instead unfold in movements, a phased approach that allows the melody of progress to resonate, even when the orchestra of finances plays a restrained tune. This strategy, dividing the construction into manageable segments, permits a pause in the crescendo of spending, offering time to replenish reserves without halting the symphony of progress. Initially focusing on completing the living quarters before venturing into ancillary spaces like garages or patios allows for habitation, turning the construction site into a home, even as the remaining phases await their overture. This systematic progression through the construction acts not only as a financial strategy but as a narrative of growth, each phase a chapter that builds upon the last, culminating in a crescendo that echoes the fulfillment of dreams realized incrementally.

Negotiation with Contractors

In the orchestra of construction, the contractors and suppliers play a pivotal role; their expertise and resources are the instruments that bring the vision of a barndominium to life. Here, in the harmonious exchange of services for compensation, lies an opportunity for negotiation, a chance to fine-tune the cost without dampening the quality. Initiating this dialogue with a chorus of research and competitive quotes transforms the conversation, ensuring the negotiation unfolds from a position of knowledge and strength. Expressing flexibility in timing or material selection can harmonize the interests of both parties, often uncovering cost-saving alternatives that are independent of the project's integrity. Establishing a clear, detailed contract sets the tempo for this engagement, outlining the expectations and deliverables and ensuring that the final performance resonates with the satisfaction of value received for funds expended.

In this construction continuum, where dreams materialize from the ether of imagination to the tangible realm of the barndominium, the strategies for cost-saving without sacrificing quality emerge as constraints and liberators. They champion the cause of beauty, functionality, and sustainability, ensuring that the sanctum created stands as a testament to what is possible within the confines of a budget and to the enduring power of innovation and intention. In this space, where every choice is deliberate and every strategy infused with purpose, the barndominium rises, a monument to the belief that quality and fiscal prudence can indeed coalesce, crafting a home that is both a haven and a hallmark of wise stewardship.

DIY VS. PROFESSIONAL COSTS: MAKING INFORMED DECISIONS

In the nuanced ballet of constructing a barndominium, homeowners find themselves at the confluence of aspiration and pragmatism, where the allure of personal craftsmanship meets the precision of professional expertise. This intersection demands a discerning approach to decision-making and a calibration of ambitions against the backdrop of skill, time, and financial resources.

Assessing DIY Potential

Embarking on DIY endeavors within the barndominium construction or renovation requires an introspective gaze into one's repertoire of skills and the depth of one's commitment. It is a realm where enthusiasm must be matched by aptitude and where the complexity of tasks ranges from the mundane to the arcane. For those with a penchant for craftsmanship, more straightforward projects like painting, basic carpentry, or even the installation of fixtures fall well within the ambit of achievable tasks. However, this self-assessment extends beyond identifying capabilities; it encompasses the willingness to learn, the resilience to endure trial and error challenges, and the temporal bandwidth to see projects to fruition. This introspection is not merely about cataloging existing skills but about charting a realistic path through the construction process that acknowledges both limitations and potential for growth.

Calculating True Costs of DIY

The calculus of DIY, often perceived through the lens of material savings, necessitates a broader perspective that accounts for the currency of time and the potential for missteps. Actual costs extend beyond the price of materials, enveloping the investment of hours that might otherwise be spent in pursuits of leisure or professional endeavors. Moreover, the equation must factor in the learning curve, the tools required for the task, and, critically, the cost of rectifying errors. Misjudged cuts, improper installations, or suboptimal finishes detract from the barndominium's aesthetic and functional integrity and necessitate additional expenditure, either in rework materials or professional fees, to correct the faults. Thus, the financial ledger of DIY projects must account for these variables, offering a holistic view that informs decision-making beyond the initial allure of cost savings.

When to Hire Professionals

Safety, compliance, and complexity considerations guide the decision to enlist professionals. Tasks that interface with the barndominium's structural integrity, electrical systems, and plumbing demand specialized knowledge and adherence to codes and standards that govern safety and functionality. Professionals bring to the table not only their expertise but also their credentials, ensuring that the work performed meets the rigorous demands of building inspectors and the implicit trust of future inhabitants. Moreover, complex installations that require precision, specialized tools, or certifications—such as HVAC systems or custom cabinetry— warrant professional engagement. In these instances, the value derived from hiring experts transcends the simplicity of task completion, embedding within the project a level of craftsmanship and reliability that DIY efforts might not reliably replicate.

Balancing DIY and Professional Work

The orchestration of a barndominium's construction as a harmonious blend of DIY and professional contributions is an exercise in strategic planning and humility. It begins with a map of the project's scope, allocating tasks along the spectrum of complexity and personal capability. Here, a phased approach emerges as a strategy, allowing for professional work to lay the foundation upon which DIY projects can be built, ensuring that tasks are approached in a logical sequence that respects the integrity of the construction process. This strategy not only maximizes budget efficiency but also elevates the quality of the finished home, ensuring that each element, whether born of professional expertise or DIY dedication, contributes to a cohesive whole.

Moreover, this balance fosters a collaborative spirit, where homeowners and professionals engage in a dialogue of creation, each learning from the other. Homeowners gain insights into the nuances of construction, accruing skills, and knowledge that enrich their DIY endeavors. Conversely, professionals, informed by the homeowner's vision and direct involvement, are better positioned to tailor their contributions to the project's aesthetic and functional goals. This synergy, a confluence of perspectives and skills, cultivates an environment where the act of building becomes more than the sum of its parts, transforming the process into a journey of shared achievement and collective pride.

In this landscape, where the barndominium rises as a testament to the fusion of dreams and pragmatism, the outline between DIY and professional work becomes less of a boundary than a bridge. It connects the realms of personal capability and expert proficiency, ensuring that each step taken toward completion is informed, intentional, and imbued with the essence of collaboration. Through this lens, the construction of a barndominium transcends the act of building, evolving into an odyssey of learning, creating, and becoming, where every decision, every nail is driven, and every brushstroke is a reflection of a more profound journey toward crafting, not just a space, but a sanctuary that resonates with the harmonies of home.

LONG-TERM SAVINGS: ENERGY-EFFICIENT DESIGN AND MATERIALS

In the intricate dance of constructing a barndominium, the melody of immediate costs often drowns out the quieter yet persistent harmony of long-term savings. Within this nuanced interplay, the virtues of energy-efficient design and materials emerge, not merely as facets of modern construction but as pillars of a sustainable future. While seemingly steep, the initial investment in such innovations paves a golden path to substantial savings, a testament to the adage that the actual cost of a home is not in its building but in its dwelling.

The narrative of energy efficiency begins with the deliberate selection of systems that promise a reduction in the barndominium's thirst for energy. Heating, cooling, and electrical frameworks, the lifelines of domestic comfort, are scrutinized for their efficiency ratings. Heat pumps, celebrated for their ability to draw warmth from the air or ground, offer a ballet of heating and cooling in one, sidestepping the energy-intensive performances of traditional systems. Similarly, modern HVAC systems, with their sophisticated zoning and programmable thermostats, whisper a tale of tailored climates, reducing the wasteful chorus of heating unoccupied spaces. The choice extends into appliances and lighting, where ENERGY STAR-rated wares and LED bulbs stand as champions of efficiency, their presence in the home a constant, gentle pressure on the pulse of energy consumption.

Yet, the quest for efficiency is not solely in selecting systems but in embracing materials and methods that fortify the barndominium against the elements. High-quality insulation, a silent guardian in the walls, floors, and ceilings, repels the extremes of outside temperatures, its effectiveness measured in the whisper of the furnace or the silence of the air conditioner. The art of sealing, meticulous and often overlooked, finds its stage around windows, doors, and junctions, a performance of caulks and weather-stripping that banishes drafts and whispers tales of uninterrupted comfort. Together, these choices form an unbroken seal, a barrier against the whims of weather and the tyranny of thermal exchange.

Amid this symphony of efficiency, the chorus of government incentives rises, a melody of financial support for those who choose the path of energy conservation. Tax credits, rebates, and grants, each a note in the harmony of encouragement, offer a reduction in the upfront costs associated with energy-efficient design and materials. These incentives, varying in scope and scale across regions, serve as a beacon, guiding homeowners toward choices that align with personal economy and ecological stewardship. For those who listen closely, these programs unravel the complexities of initial investment, revealing a landscape where the promise of future savings and environmental preservation mitigates the cost of energy-efficient upgrades.

In this narrative, where the construction of a barndominium unfolds as an ode to sustainability and foresight, the emphasis on energy-efficient design and materials transcends the immediate. It becomes a legacy, a testament to a vision that values not just the aesthetics and functionality of a home but its role in a larger ecological and economic context. This approach, marked by careful selection and strategic investment, ensures that the barndominium stands not as a monument to excess but as a beacon of balance, where the harmony of living comfortably and sustainably resonates through its halls.

INSURANCE AND WARRANTIES: PROTECTING YOUR INVESTMENT

Navigating Construction Insurance

In the intricate canvas of barndominium construction, insurance emerges not as a mere technicality but as a foundational element, a safeguard against the unpredictable whims of fate and circumstance.

At the heart of this protective measure lies a spectrum of policies, each tailored to shield against specific vulnerabilities inherent in the building process. Builder's risk insurance, for instance, stands as a bulwark against damage to the property during construction, covering perils from fire and theft to natural disasters. Its scope, customizable to the project's duration and value, ensures a safety net encapsulating the material and labor investment.

Liability insurance, conversely, addresses the human element, offering protection against claims of injury or property damage caused by construction activities. This policy becomes crucial in an era where litigation can arise from unforeseen accidents, securing peace of mind for both the homeowner and the on-site workforce. For those navigating the waters of subcontracting, ensuring that each entity brings its coverage to the project's tapestry is vital. It creates a composite shield that leaves no thread of risk exposed.

Navigating this labyrinth requires a meticulous approach and a dialogue with insurance professionals who can tailor policies to the project's unique landscape. Such conversations should delve into the specifics of coverage limits, deductibles, and exclusions, ensuring clarity on what scenarios are encapsulated within the protective embrace of the policy. While initially perceived as a foray into a world of complexities, this proactive engagement with insurance ultimately weaves a safety net that allows the creative spirit of barndominium construction to flourish, unhampered by the specter of financial risk.

Homeowner's Insurance for Barndominiums

Securing homeowner's insurance for barndominiums unfolds as a narrative distinct from traditional homes, reflecting these versatile structures' unique characteristics and uses. The hybrid nature of barndominiums, often straddling the line between residential and commercial or agricultural use, necessitates a policy that comprehends this duality. Insurers may tread cautiously, prompted by the unconventional aspects of barndominium living, from incorporating large workshops or garages to adapting industrial materials for residential purposes.

This journey toward securing coverage demands transparency and detailed documentation, presenting insurers with comprehensive insights into the barndominium's construction, use, and safety features. Enhanced security systems, fire suppression technologies, and adherence to building codes mitigate the perceived risk and can tilt the scales toward more favorable premiums. In certain instances, engaging specialized insurance providers who understand and appreciate the unique value proposition of barndominiums becomes necessary, forging a partnership that recognizes the structure's worth beyond conventional metrics.

The quest for adequate coverage is repetitious, a negotiation that balances the insurer's need for risk management with the homeowner's desire for comprehensive protection. It is a dialogue punctuated by questions of value, replacement costs, and liability coverage, each query a step toward a policy that encapsulates the barndominium's essence while safeguarding the owner's investment.

Understanding Warranties

Warranties in the realm of barndominium construction serve as a testament to the quality and a promise of durability, offering reassurance beyond the mere completion of the build. Builder warranties, typically spanning a year, cover labor and materials, addressing potential defects that might emerge in the nascent stages of the home's life. Extended warranties, while less common, delve deeper, safeguarding structural elements for a decade or more, ensuring that the foundation upon which dreams are built remains unshaken.

The discernment of these warranties' value lies in the details, in the fine print that defines the boundaries of coverage. Homeowners must navigate these documents critically, probing for clarity on what is included, the claims process, and the dispute resolution mechanisms. This scrutiny ensures that the warranty serves its intended purpose, not as a mere marketing tool but as a genuine layer of protection that complements the insurance framework.

Engagement with builders on this topic should be forthright. They should seek not just to understand the warranty offered but also to compare it against industry standards. This conversation, while potentially delicate, is essential. It ensures that the warranty reflects the quality of the craftsmanship and the materials, offering peace of mind that the investment is protected against visible and latent defects.

Risk Management Strategies

Strategies for managing risks throughout the barndominium construction process emerge not as afterthoughts but as integral components of project planning. This proactive approach to risk management begins with selecting reputable builders and subcontractors whose expertise and ethical practices lay a foundation of trust and quality. Rigorous contract review, ensuring clarity on responsibilities, timelines, and recourse in case of discrepancies, further mitigates potential conflicts, embedding a legal framework that supports project integrity.

On-site safety protocols, from regular inspections to adherence to safety regulations, minimize the likelihood of accidents, protect workers, and reduce the risk of liability claims.

Documentation plays a pivotal role in this strategy, with detailed records of inspections, permits, and communications as a bulwark against misunderstandings or disputes.

This multifaceted approach to risk management, blending legal, operational, and ethical strategies, ensures a construction process that aims to minimize the need for insurance claims and fosters an environment where creativity and innovation can thrive, unfettered by the constraints of unresolved risks.

PROPERTY TAXES AND YOUR BARNDOMINIUM: WHAT TO EXPECT

Within the intricate landscape of barndominium ownership, the aspect of property taxes intricately intertwines—a consistently fluctuating expense necessitating careful consideration and comprehension. The assessment and valuation of these unique dwellings for tax purposes differs from the method used for traditional residences, reflecting their distinctive nature and multifunctional use. This divergence often stems from the dual-purpose design of barndominiums, serving as a domicile and, in many instances, a space for agriculture or business. Tax assessors approach these properties with a lens that attempts to quantify their residential and utilitarian aspects separately. This may yield a valuation mosaic reflective of the barndominium's composite parts rather than its holistic worth.

The underpinning of property tax assessment lies in determining a barndominium's market value and estimating its worth in a free and open market. This valuation considers various factors, including location, size, and construction specifics, such as materials and architectural design. Comparables, or "comps," properties with similar characteristics and uses in the vicinity, play a significant role in this assessment. However, the rarity and unique customization of many barndominiums can challenge this comparison, leading to assessments that may not fully encapsulate the property's personalized nature.

Strategies to navigate and potentially minimize property taxes emerge as pivotal for owners, blending legal shrewdness with a strategic understanding of local tax codes. Agricultural exemptions, where applicable, offer a significant avenue for reduction, recognizing the portion of the barndominium used for farming or livestock as contributing to the state's agricultural output. This exemption, however, necessitates a demonstrable engagement in farming activities, subject to specific local criteria that might include land size and use intensity. Similarly, homestead exemptions provide relief for the portion of the barndominium serving as the primary residence, a testament to policies designed to encourage homeownership and stabilize communities.

The labyrinth of tax implications surrounding barndominium ownership extends beyond the annual assessment, touching on development and future planning aspects. Capital improvements, for example, may increase a property's assessed value, influencing future tax liabilities. Owners find themselves balancing the desire for enhancements against the potential for increased taxation, a calculation that requires foresight and, often, consultation with property tax professionals. In this realm, understanding the shades of tax codes becomes not just beneficial but essential, offering insights into how improvements can be planned and executed to align with both the vision for the property and the imperative of fiscal prudence.

When assessments that seem disproportionately high reflect neither the barndominium's market value nor its use accurately, the avenue of appeal opens. Formal and driven by deadlines, this process requires a meticulous compilation of evidence that challenges the assessor's valuation. Documentation, from detailed descriptions of the property and its uses to photographs and comparables that accurately reflect its value, becomes the currency of persuasion in these appeals. Professional appraisals may further bolster the case, providing an expert valuation that counters the assessment. Navigating this appeal process demands a comprehensive understanding of the barndominium's value and an articulate presentation of the case, often within the context of local tax board hearings.

In this intricate dance with property taxes, barndominium owners tread a path that intertwines with legal statutes, market valuations, and personal advocacy. The challenge lies not in the certainty of taxation but in ensuring that assessments accurately reflect the property's true essence and use. Through strategic planning, legal utilization of exemptions, and vigilant readiness to appeal when necessary, owners can navigate the fiscal landscape, ensuring that their barndominium remains a haven of personal and financial fulfillment. While complex, this engagement with the intricacies of property taxes underscores the broader commitment to stewardship of the barndominium, affirming its place not just as a structure but as a pivotal component of its owner's life and legacy.

FINANCIAL PLANNING POST-CONSTRUCTION

In the aftermath of construction, the financial planning land-scape for a barndominium owner transforms, presenting new terrains to navigate and opportunities to cultivate. This phase, often overshadowed by the immediacy of building costs, unfolds as a critical period where strategic financial decisions lay the groundwork for enduring value and sustainability.

Budgeting for Maintenance and Upkeep

The art of budgeting for the ongoing maintenance and upkeep of a barndominium requires understanding the property's needs and the cyclic nature of care it demands. Allocating funds for future repairs begins with a detailed assessment of the home's components, from the hardiness of its structure to the efficiency of its systems. A systematic approach involves setting aside a portion of monthly expenses into a dedicated maintenance fund, a reservoir from which resources can be drawn to address both the expected and the unforeseen wear of time. This proactive stance mitigates the impact of repairs on the household's financial equilibrium and preserves the barndominium's integrity and appeal.

Equally, acknowledging that certain elements, like HVAC systems or roofing, have limited lifespans prompts an antici-patory saving strategy. By projecting these components' replacement timelines and costs, owners can diffuse the financial burden over the years, transforming substantial outlays into manageable, incremental savings. This foresight, coupled with regular inspections and maintenance, prolongs the life of the home's critical systems, ensuring their operation remains both efficient and cost-effective.

Refinancing Options

Post-construction, the barndominium's increased value and the owner's equity present a lattice of refinancing options, each with the potential to optimize financial terms or unlock liquidity for future endeavors. For many, refinancing goals converge on securing lower interest rates, a shift that can significantly reduce monthly mortgage payments and total interest paid over the loan's life. Others might find value in adjusting the loan's term, shortening it to build equity more rapidly, or extending it to ease monthly financial pressures.

This exploration of refinancing options necessitates a comprehensive market analysis, comparing current rates and terms against the existing mortgage. Engaging in this process with a clear objective and an understanding of the costs involved, from closing fees to potential penalties, ensures that the decision to refinance is grounded in its net benefit to the homeowner's financial landscape.

Long-Term Financial Considerations

Beyond the immediate horizon of maintenance and refinancing, long-term financial considerations for barndominium owners weave into the broader tapestry of wealth management and legacy planning. The barndominium, as an asset, stands within the owner's portfolio not merely as a domicile but as a vehicle for wealth accumulation and, potentially, generational transfer. Nurturing its value through careful upkeep and strategic improvements ensures it appreciates over time, bolstering the owner's net worth.

In parallel, estate planning emerges as a pivotal component of this long-term view, ensuring that the barndominium's value is preserved and transferred according to the owner's wishes. Instruments like trusts or life estates offer mechanisms through which ownership can be structured to provide for heirs while minimizing exposure to probate or estate taxes. This foresight ensures that the barndominium's legacy, as a cherished space and a financial asset, endures, reflecting the owner's intentions and care.

Maximizing Your Investment

Maximizing the return on investment in a barndominium transcends the pursuit of financial gain, capturing a spectrum of rewards that span the tangible to the intangible. Rental income, whether from long-term leases or short-term hospitality ventures, presents a direct avenue for monetizing the property's value, leveraging its appeal and functionality to generate a steady income stream. This approach capitalizes on the barndominium's unique attributes and introduces it to a larger audience, enhancing its profile and potential market value.

On the resale front, strategic improvements that boost the barndominium's aesthetic appeal or functional utility can significantly impact its attractiveness to potential buyers, commanding a premium in the market. Yet, beyond these monetary metrics, the investment in a barndominium yields dividends in the quality of life it affords, the memories it hosts, and the sense of place it nurtures. Although challenging to quantify, these non-material benefits significantly enhance the owner's overall return on investment by enriching the barndominium's living experience.

As this chapter integrates into the broader narrative of barndominium ownership, it underscores the importance of proactive financial supervision in all phases, from construction to legacy planning. The strategies and considerations outlined here serve not only as a guide for navigating the post-construction financial landscape but also as a reflection on the multi-layered value of the barndominium. It is a testament to the vision and effort invested in its creation, a beacon of personal fulfillment, and a cornerstone of financial strategy. As we move forward, the exploration persists in unraveling the dynamic connection between homeowner and residence, immersing into the patterns of barndominium living and the continual interplay among space, design, and daily life.

6

THE RHYTHMS OF BARNDOMINIUM LIVING

A barndominium, with its sprawling open spaces and rustic charm blended with modern amenities, presents a canvas for a lifestyle redefined. This shift in habitat, from the conventional to the extraordinary, nudges us to recalibrate our daily rhythms, inviting an alignment with the expansive and the sustainable. It's not merely about inhabiting a space; it's about embracing a lifestyle harmonizing with our aspirations and values.

TRANSITIONING TO BARNDOMINIUM LIFE: A GUIDE

Adjusting Expectations

The transition from traditional homes to a barndominium's unique setting entails an adjustment period, where the familiar contours of compartmentalized rooms give way to the grandeur of open spaces. This shift might initially unsettle the rhythm of daily life, where activities once confined to specific rooms now flow into one another. It's similar to adjusting to the acoustics of a new instrument, where the notes played remain the same but resonate differently. In a barndominium, the morning coffee brewed in the kitchen seamlessly blends into the workspace with only a few steps, eliminating the boundaries that once categorized our lives. This liberating fluidity requires a mental shift, embracing openness as a channel for creativity and connection rather than an expanse of emptiness.

Embracing Open Spaces

The hallmark of barndominium living lies in its open spaces, which require a thoughtful approach to maximize their potential for both daily living and special occasions. For instance, strategically placing furniture can create invisible boundaries that define functional areas without erecting barriers. A well-placed bookshelf becomes a distinction between the living area and a study, offering privacy without isolation. During gatherings, these spaces transform, the bookshelf serving not just as a library but as a backdrop for conversations and camaraderie. This adaptability extends to incorporating indoor and outdoor living, where large sliding doors erase the line between inside and out, expanding the living space to embrace the natural world.

Community Integration

Integrating into the local community becomes a pivotal aspect of the transition for those transitioning from urban environments to the more rural settings where barndominiums often nestle. This integration is less about assimilation and more about finding common ground, a shared appreciation for the landscape and its rhythms. Participation in local farmers' markets, volunteering for community projects, or joining local clubs can serve as bridges, connecting new residents with their neighbors. These activities embed individuals within the social fabric of their new locale, intertwining their stories with those of the community and fostering a sense of belonging rooted in mutual respect and shared experiences.

Sustainable Living Practices

Barndominiums, by their very nature, lend themselves to sustainable living practices. The expansive spaces and connection to the land invite a lifestyle that prioritizes harmony with the environment. Rainwater harvesting systems can be integrated to collect water for landscaping or agricultural uses, reducing reliance on municipal sources. Solar panels, installed on the vast roof areas these structures often boast, can significantly offset energy costs, their presence a testament to a commitment to renewable energy. Composting and vegetable gardening further this ethos, turning waste into resources and providing sustenance that travels only from garden to table. This alignment with sustainable practices reduces the environmental footprint of the barndominium but also instills a deep sense of stewardship and connection to the land.

Sustainable Living Checklist

To foster a seamless transition into sustainable barndominium living, consider the following:

- Assess the potential for solar panel installation, considering roof space and sun exposure.
- Explore rainwater harvesting systems suited to the property's size and the region's rainfall patterns.
- Initiate a composting system to reduce waste and enrich the soil.
- Plan a vegetable garden, selecting crops suited to the local climate and soil conditions.
- Investigate local recycling programs and participate actively.
- Consider the installation of energy-efficient appliances and LED lighting.
- Research sustainable building materials for any future renovations or additions.

This checklist serves as a foundation, a starting point for integrating sustainable practices into the textile of barndominium living, transforming daily routines into acts of environmental guardianship.

Navigating the transition to barndominium life, one encounters a landscape ripe with opportunities for growth, connection, and sustainable living. This lifestyle is not confined but liberating, offering expanses to redefine the contours of home and community. It invites an engagement with the mindful and enriching environment, fostering a harmony that resonates throughout daily life.

MAINTAINING YOUR BARNDOMINIUM: ROUTINE UPKEEP AND SEASONAL TASKS

Within the domain of barndominium living, the cadence of maintenance echoes persistently, consistently reminding us that the allure and functionality of these distinctive structures demand steadfast and continuous dedication. Beyond the allure of their spacious interiors and the blend of rustic and modern aesthetics lies a reality grounded in the practicalities of upkeep and the foresight of seasonal preparedness. This section unfolds as a guide to navigating these responsibilities, ensuring that the barndominium remains a fortress of comfort and durability through the years.

Regular Maintenance Schedule

Developing a routine for regular maintenance tasks is the primary strategy to combat the inevitable wear and tear that time and usage inflict. This meticulously designed schedule encompasses various activities, each critical to preserving the barndominium's integrity. Weekly cleaning rituals focused on dust and debris removal prevent the accumulation that can lead to wear on surfaces and fixtures. Monthly inspections of HVAC filters, a seemingly minor task, play a pivotal role in ensuring the efficiency and longevity of climate control systems, a heartbeat within the home's larger organism. The focus shifts to the exterior; quarterly maintenance is when gutter clearance and window seal inspections prevent water ingress, the subtle yet insidious enemy of structural health. While rigorous, this elevated level of care imbues the homeowner with a profound connection to the space, each task a step in a dance of preservation and pride.

Seasonal Preparations

As the seasons turn, so does the focus of maintenance, a shift that anticipates each period's unique challenges. In the embrace of winter, the barndominium requires fortification against the cold, a process that begins with plumbing winterizing to guard against the freeze and fracture of pipes, an ordeal that can lead to significant damage. The approach of summer, with its promise of heat and potential for wildfires, demands preparations, including clearing brush and inspecting firebreaks, ensuring the home stands resilient against nature's fiercer moods. This seasonal pivot in maintenance tasks safeguards the barndominium against the elements and serves as a ritual, marking time and change within the home's constant.

Long-Term Care

Beyond the cyclical demands of routine and seasonal maintenance lies the realm of long-term care. This vision projects into the future, anticipating the needs of a structure intended to endure. Central to this vision is the inspection of the roof, a watchman against the elements, where biennial checks seek out potential breaches or wear that could compromise the home's sheltering purpose. Similarly, the periodic application of exterior paint refreshes the barndominium's aesthetic and serves as a protective skin, shielding against moisture and the sun's relentless gaze. Though less frequent, these acts of long-term care are foundational to the barndominium's longevity, ensuring that it remains a place of residence with a legacy of resilience and beauty.

DIY Maintenance Tips

For the barndominium owner, the call to hands-on involvement in the home's maintenance is practical and deeply personal, a manifestation of care and connection to the space. Simple tasks, such as tightening loose fixtures or applying caulk to seal gaps, empower owners to contribute directly to their home's upkeep. Creating a personalized maintenance kit equipped with the tools and materials for everyday tasks prepares the owner for the inevitable minor repairs and adjustments that a lived-in space demands. This DIY approach fosters a deeper understanding and appreciation of the barndominium's workings and cultivates a sense of capability and independence, which echo the very spirit of barndominium living.

In keeping a barndominium, the commitment to maintenance is both a duty and a privilege, reflecting a broader ethos of care and sustainability. This engagement with the practical aspects of upkeep, from the daily to the seasonal, from the immediate to the long-term, knit a thread of continuity and affection through the fabric of barndominium living. In this meticulous attention to care, the barndominium transcends its physical form, becoming a living testament to the values of durability, beauty, and the enduring human touch.

UPGRADING AND RENOVATING YOUR SPACE

Within the expansive embrace of a barndominium lies a canvas ripe for evolution, a space where the pulse of creativity propels us toward transformation. Upgrading and renovating these unique dwellings requires more than a blueprint; it demands a symphony of imagination, pragmatism, and reverence for the structure's inherent character. Here, in the experimentation of change, we find an opportunity to enhance our living environment and reaffirm our connection to the essence of our home.

Planning Your Upgrades

The genesis of any renovation project begins with a vision that connects desire with feasibility. In this context, planning is an exercise in precision, where each decision is weighed against the backdrop of the barndominium's architectural soul. To preserve this essence, one must tread lightly, ensuring that updates amplify rather than mute the structure's intrinsic charm. Meticulous preparation is the key to striking this delicate balance, where aesthetic aspirations harmonize flawlessly with structural integrity. A dialogue with history, acknowledging the original purpose and form of the barndominium, guides this process, ensuring that the narrative continuity is preserved. Effective planning thus becomes a bridge between past and future, a respectful nod to tradition coupled with an eager glance toward innovation.

Cost-Effective Upgrades

In the realm of renovation, impact and cost do not always correlate. Strategic upgrades, chosen for their ability to alter a space's perception and functionality significantly, can be modest and transformative. The introduction of skylights, for instance, invites the dance of daylight, changing the ambiance of interiors without the need for structural upheaval. Similarly, replacing traditional insulation with green alternatives offers enhanced energy efficiency and environmental charge while maintaining fiscal prudence. These thoughtfully chosen interventions reflect a philosophy of deliberate improvement, where each modification serves multiple purposes by combining utility with aesthetic enhancement.

Navigating Permits and Regulations

The path to transformation is often lined with regulatory oversight, a necessary engagement with the frameworks that ensure safety and community harmony. Navigating this terrain requires an understanding of local codes and permits, a prerequisite that safeguards the integrity of the renovation process. This journey through bureaucracy, while sometimes daunting, is facilitated by thorough research and proactive communication with local authorities. The aim here is not merely compliance but also the cultivation of a partnership with regulatory bodies. This alliance ensures the barndominium's evolution is legally sound and aligned with community standards. It is within this careful negotiation of rules and vision that renovations find solid ground, allowing for a seamless transition from concept to reality.

Incorporating Technology

The infusion of modern technology into the fabric of a barndominium is a testament to the structure's adaptability, a nod to the future embedded within the rustic charm of the past. Smart home systems, offering control over lighting, climate, and security, introduce a previously unimagined layer of convenience and efficiency. These digital enhancements, integrated with sensitivity to the barndominium's aesthetic, bridge the gap between traditional architecture and contemporary living. Selecting technologies based on their utility and unobtrusiveness ensures that they enhance rather than overshadow the home's character. This harmonious blend of old and new, where technology serves rather than dictates the living experience, enriches the barndominium lifestyle, offering a living space that is not only beautiful but also intelligently responsive to the needs of its inhabitants.

In upgrading and renovating a barndominium, the challenges of planning, cost management, regulatory navigation, and technology integration converge. Yet, within this very union, that opportunity blooms, and it is a chance to reimagine and reshape our dwellings in ways that honor their essence while embracing the potential for change. This process, steeped in respect for the past and anticipation for the future, reaffirms our bond with our homes, transforming them into reflections of our evolving lives and aspirations. Through careful consideration and strategic action, our barndominiums remain not just places of residence but supporters of personal expression and innovation, standing as testaments to the enduring allure of transformation.

ENERGY AND UTILITY MANAGEMENT FOR EFFICIENCY

Within the tranquil haven of a barndominium, where rustic charm intertwines with refined elegance, the management of energy and utilities unfolds like a carefully choreographed ballet—a graceful performance of intentional decisions and innovations that collectively lead toward a lifestyle that is both efficient and harmonious with the rhythms of nature. This dedication to efficiency extends beyond merely adopting isolated technologies or strategies; it involves integrating them seamlessly into daily life, fostering a living environment characterized by sustainability and mindfulness.

Monitoring Energy Usage

The vigilant monitoring of energy usage within the barndominium's walls becomes the first step in a larger conservation strategy. This vigilance is empowered by the advent of smart home technologies, which serve as the eyes and ears of energy management, offering real-time insights into consumption patterns. Devices that track usage across the spectrum of household activities, from the hum of appliances to the glow of lighting, furnish data that, when carefully analyzed, reveal the contours of waste and efficiency. Armed with this knowledge, the homeowner can initiate targeted interventions—dimming lights here, adjusting the thermostat there—all orchestrated through the central nervous system of a smart home hub. This approach reduces consumption and elevates the homeowner to the role of conductor, guiding the household's energy symphony with a deft hand.

Utility Savings Plans

The selection of utility plans and providers for a barndominium transcends conventional comparison shopping, morphing into a strategic endeavor that considers the unique demands and opportunities of such a dwelling. In this quest, the barndominium's specific needs—the higher electrical demands of a workshop or the seasonal fluctuations of a rural setting—become the compass guiding the search. Providers are evaluated not just on the cost per kilowatt-hour or cubic foot of water but on their capacity to offer plans that flex with the barndominium's rhythms, perhaps offering lower rates during off-peak hours or incentives for reduced consumption. This careful matchmaking between need and offer ensures that utility costs are not merely an expense but an investment in a sustainable lifestyle, where the principles of efficiency and conservation are echoed in the monthly bills.

Renewable Energy Options

The exploration of renewable energy options for the barndominium emerges as a dialogue with the future, a conversation between present needs and the vision of a self-sustaining home. Solar panels transform sunlight into electricity with their silent magic, becoming a prominent ally in this quest. Their installation on the barndominium's ample roof spaces harnesses the sun's bounty and proclaims a commitment to renewable sources. Wind turbines, where geography permits, offer another avenue, their blades a testament to the power of the unseen wind. Once the domain of environmental enthusiasts, these technologies have evolved into practical solutions for the average homeowner, with their adoption reflecting a sense of responsibility and forward-thinking. By integrating these sources, the barndominium steps lightly upon the earth, drawing from its abundance with gratitude and care.

Water Conservation

In water stewardship, the barndominium becomes an oasis of conservation, where every drop is valued, and nothing is wasted. Rainwater harvesting systems, simple yet profoundly effective, capture the tears of the sky, redirecting them from gutters to storage tanks. This harvested bounty, once treated, can fulfill various household needs, from irrigation to washing, reducing the demand for municipal sources or wells in the landscape that cradles the barndominium, efficient landscaping practices—xeriscaping, native plants, and drip irrigation—further the cause of conservation. These practices do not merely reduce water usage; they create a harmony between the dwelling and its natural surroundings, fostering a landscape that thrives on minimal intervention.

In this domain, where the barndominium stands as a citadel of efficiency and sustainability, the management of energy and utilities unfolds as a testament to the possible—a demonstration of how mindful living and technological innovation can converge to create a home that is both a haven and a beacon of environmental administration. Through careful monitoring, strategic utility selection, the embrace of renewable energy, and water conservation, the barndominium becomes more than a place of residence; it evolves into a living example of how we might inhabit our world with grace and care, ensuring its bounty endures for generations to come.

COMMUNITY AND NEIGHBORS: FOSTERING RELATIONSHIPS

Within a barndominium's essence, community threads interlace with the daily fabric of existence, uniting individuals into a rich tapestry of shared experiences and mutual support. This interconnectedness, especially pronounced in the pastoral expanses where many such homes stand, becomes a cornerstone upon which the rhythms of barndominium life are built. Cultivating relationships with neighbors and the broader community transforms the physicality of dwelling into the warmth of belonging, an alchemy that enriches life beyond the confines of sturdy walls and open spaces.

Building Community Connections

The initiation of connections within the community transcends mere acquaintance, evolving into a deliberate act of weaving oneself into the local social fabric. This endeavor, pursued with intention and openness, taps into the communal spirit that often thrives in rural settings, where the closeness of shared values and collective resilience bridges the distances between homes. The introduction, whether through a simple greeting or the sharing of a meal, marks the beginning of this integration, a step that signals willingness to partake in the communal dance of give and take. Regular interactions, marked by genuine interest and participation in the daily lives of neighbors, gradually layer these initial connections with depth and warmth, fostering bonds that stand resilient against the deviation of time and circumstance.

Participating in Local Events

Engagement in local events is a vibrant avenue through which the barndominium dweller becomes an active participant in the community's heartbeat. These gatherings, be they festivals celebrating the harvest, markets showcasing local craftsmanship, or meetings convened to chart the community's future, serve as stages upon which the individual and the collective come together. Participation in these events deepens one's understanding of the local culture and traditions and offers opportunities to contribute talents and perspectives, enriching the communal tapestry with new patterns and hues. The presence and involvement of barndominium residents in these communal milestones underscore a commitment to collective well-being, a signal that they are not mere observers but co-creators of the community narrative.

Creating a Support Network

Establishing a support network among neighbors transcends traditional notions of community, creating a web of mutual assistance that provides a safety net for all members. This network, grounded in recognizing shared vulnerabilities and strengths, becomes a dynamic resource in times of need, whether for assistance in maintenance endeavors, support during personal trials, or collective action in emergency preparedness. Sharing skills and resources, from the mechanical knowledge required for farm equipment repairs to the culinary skills demonstrated during community meals, bolsters individual households and the community. In this environment, the barndominium becomes a node in a more extensive system of support, its residents both beneficiaries and contributors to a network that embodies the true essence of community: interdependence and shared strength.

Respecting Local Traditions

Immersing in local traditions and cultures offers a rich soil where the roots of belonging can be deeply entrenched. This respect for the established ways of life, the rituals, and practices that have shaped the community's identity signals a willingness to coexist and truly understand and honor the heritage that precedes one's arrival. Participation in these traditions, whether it involves learning the steps of a folk dance, contributing to the communal harvest, or observing local customs with reverence, becomes an act of homage to the community's ancestors and a pledge to carry their legacy. Through this respectful engagement, the newcomer, once an outsider, becomes woven into the community fabric, their presence acknowledged not as an imposition but as a valuable thread in the continuing story of the place.

In this intricate dance of fostering relationships within the community and with neighbors, the barndominium dweller finds a sense of belonging and a deeper engagement with the essence of communal living. It is here, in the interplay of building connections, participating in local events, creating support networks, and respecting traditions, that the barndominium becomes more than a home; it transforms into a living testament to the power of community, a beacon of interconnectedness that enriches every aspect of life within its walls and beyond. This journey, pursued with intention and open-heartedness, ensures that the barndominium stands not in isolation but as an integral part of a vibrant, supportive, and enduring community.

THE IMPACT OF BARNDOMINIUM LIVING ON WELL-BEING

Immersion in the barndominium lifestyle brings forth an intricate tapestry where the threads of human wellness are interwoven with the natural and communal environment, crafting a narrative where health and habitat resonate with profound synergy. This existence, marked by closeness to nature, thoughtful design, vibrant community ties, and a harmonious work-life balance, cultivates a realm where well-being flourishes, nurtured by the surroundings and the lifestyle it engenders.

In the embrace of nature, which the barndominium life so generously offers, there lies a potent balm for the weary spirit and a tonic for the tired body. The mere act of gazing out upon a landscape where the horizon stretches wide, unfettered by the confines of urban sprawl, widens the stress-narrowed channels of our being, inviting tranquility to flow through the open spaces within us. This connection, unconscious and immediate, to the living tapestry outside our windows—where mornings are heralded by the chorus of birds and the air is vibrant with the hum of life—rekindles a primal bond with the natural world, a relationship known to enhance both mental clarity and emotional equilibrium. Studies, though not cited here directly, have long affirmed the beneficial effects of such communion with nature, linking it to reduced levels of anxiety, heightened feelings of happiness, and an overall enhancement in life satisfaction.

The sanctuaries we create within our barndominiums, designed with well-being at their core, reflect a conscious choice to infuse our living spaces with elements that nourish both body and soul. Spaces dedicated to meditation or exercise become sacred groves for self-care, where the architecture around us supports the pursuit of physical health and mental serenity. Designating spaces for these activities, suffused with natural light and providing vistas of the serene surroundings, encourages a daily wellness embrace. Within these sacred areas, the boundaries between physical exertion and mental serenity fade away, nurturing holistic health that extends its influence across all facets of barndominium life.

The tightly woven community surrounding the barndominium residents is a crucial element in the tapestry of well-being. In this communal dance, each participant contributes to a collective resilience that buffers against the isolating tendencies of modern existence through acts of sharing, support, and social engagement. This interdependence, a hallmark of barndominium communities, fosters a sense of belonging and shared identity, which are indispensable to psychological health. The richness of these social connections, cultivated in gatherings, shared projects, and simple day-to-day exchanges, imbues life with a sense of purpose and belonging, counteracting the alienation that often shadows contemporary life.

For those who have integrated their professional pursuits into their barndominium lifestyle, finding a balance between work and life becomes a significant challenge, albeit one ripe with opportunities for cultivating a fulfilling existence. The design of a barndominium, inherently flexible, offers the physical space to separate work from leisure, an architectural cue to the psyche to transition between modes of being. When adhered to, this separation reinforces boundaries that protect personal time from the encroachment of professional obligations, a description increasingly blurred in the age of remote work. Within this framework, the discipline of structuring the day and allotting time for work, rest, and play becomes not just a schedule to be followed but a ritual that honors the multifaceted nature of human existence. This ritual, attuned to the individual rhythms of productivity and replenishment, supports a lifestyle where work is a part of life, not the consumer of it, fostering an environment where stress is managed and well-being is paramount.

In the realm of barndominium living, where the boundaries between inside and outside blur, community and solitude find their balance, and where work and leisure coexist in harmony, well-being emerges as the natural state. This lifestyle, grounded in the principles of connection, design, community, and equilibrium, offers a blueprint for living that not only sustains but enriches, a testament to the potential for a life well-lived within the embrace of a barndominium lifestyle.

HOSTING AND ENTERTAINING IN YOUR BARNDOMINIUM

In the spacious embrace of a barndominium, hosting and entertaining unfolds gracefully and quickly, where traditional homes might struggle to match. The architecture that defines these structures—a seamless blend of utility and beauty, openness and intimacy—sets the stage for gatherings that linger in guests' memories long after the last farewells are whispered.

Leveraging Open Spaces

Within the vast, open interiors, the potential for grand celebrations and cozy get-togethers awaits activation by the imaginative host. This generous layout encourages a new approach to entertainment, where the lack of walls promotes conversation and the dynamics of social interaction. Customized, adaptable, versatile furniture becomes essential in creating tailored environments suitable for the specific nature of each event. Modular sofas, easily reconfigured, invite intimate clusters for quiet conversation while long, communal tables beckon guests to dine together, sharing stories and laughter under the soft glow of reclaimed lighting fixtures. Here, the open space becomes a canvas, each gathering an opportunity to paint anew the ambiance and mood, guided by the host's vision and the unique character of the barndominium itself.

Outdoor Entertaining

The transition from the interior expanse to the beauty of the outdoor setting is fluid and natural, extending the venue for entertainment to the embrace of the surrounding landscape. Decks and patios, echoing the barndominium's aesthetic, offer vistas that frame the natural world, turning a simple sunset into a backdrop for evening soirees. Integrating outdoor kitchens and fire pits encourages a blend of culinary adventure and warmth, around which stories can unfold and connections deepen. Gardens, whether ornamental or edible, invite guests to wander, touch, and smell, engaging with the environment in a manner that indoor spaces seldom allow. This extension of the entertainment space into the outdoors reflects a lifestyle that honors the land and the sky, immersing each gathering in the beauty that encircles the barndominium.

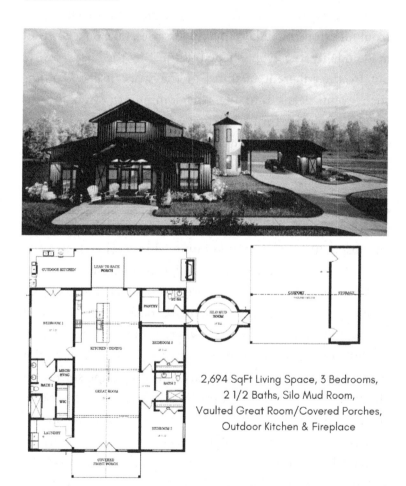

2,694 SqFt Living Space, 3 Bedrooms, 2 1/2 Baths, Silo Mud Room, Vaulted Great Room/Covered Porches, Outdoor Kitchen & Fireplace

Hosting Events and Gatherings

The versatility of the barndominium, with its open spaces and integration with the outdoors, presents a unique venue for events that range from the intimately personal to the broadly communal. Workshops and retreats find a fitting setting in the adaptive spaces of the barndominium, where the ambiance supports both focus and creativity, the natural light and expansive views fueling inspiration. Celebrations, from milestone birthdays to anniversaries, take on a custom-made quality, the event shaped not just by the host's desires but by the inherent qualities of the space itself. Planning such events leans into the barndominium's strengths—its capacity for transformation and adaptation—allowing each occasion to imprint itself upon the space, leaving echoes of laughter and joy in its wake.

Accommodating Guests

In hospitality, the barndominium shines as a beacon of warmth and welcome, and its design is inherently suited to making guests feel both impressed and at home. Guest rooms are thoughtfully appointed, balance privacy with accessibility, and offer retreats where visitors can recharge in solitude or quickly join the larger group. The consideration given to these spaces—the quality of bedding, the softness of the light, the access to nature through windows or private patios—speaks of a hospitality that seeks to accommodate and enchant. For larger gatherings, innovative solutions like convertible studios or lofted sleeping areas offer comfortable lodging, ensuring that no guest departs feeling less than cherished. This approach to guest accommodation, where every detail is attended to with care, ensures that the barn-dominium is not just a place of gathering but a haven of rest and rejuvenation for all who enter.

In the orchestration of hosting and entertaining within the barndominium, the interplay of indoor and outdoor space, the versatility of design, and the depth of consideration for guest comfort come together in a symphony of hospitality. This environment, inherently flexible and infused with the natural beauty of its setting, offers a stage upon which any event can unfold gracefully. From the grandeur of large cele-brations to the intimacy of small gatherings, the barndo-minium stands ready to accommodate, its very structure an invitation to come together, share, and revel in the joy of community and connection.

THE BARNDOMINIUM AS A LEGACY: PASSING ON YOUR HOME

In the heart of every barndominium pulses the potential for a legacy, a chance to bestow upon future generations not just a structure of wood and steel but a testament to a life lived with intention and care. This vision of the barndominium as a family homestead, enduring through the ages, requires more than the passage of keys; it demands a foresight and planning that intertwines legal wisdom with the threads of memory, sustainability, and adaptation.

Creating a Family Homestead

Envisioning your barndominium as an ancestral anchor, a homestead to be cherished and passed down, begins with imbuing the space with a sense of history and belonging. This process transcends the physical, embedding the values, stories, and aspirations that define your family in the walls. Each choice, from sustainable materials to the cultivation of the surrounding land, serves as a chapter in an ongoing narrative that speaks to this legacy's present and future caretakers. It's about crafting spaces that adapt to changing needs while retaining the essence of home, ensuring that what you pass on is more than a dwelling: it's a haven that evolves yet remains constant in its warmth and welcome.

Legal and Financial Planning

The assurance that your barndominium can transition smoothly into the hands of those who follow hinges on meticulous legal and financial planning. This journey involves navigating the complexities of estate laws, trusts, and wills, mechanisms designed to protect and preserve your legacy against the unpredictable. Engaging with legal professionals who understand the intricacies of property law becomes crucial, ensuring that your intentions for the barndominium's future are enshrined in binding documents, immune to the changes often accompanying asset transfer. Similarly, financial planning, focusing on minimizing liabilities and ensuring the homestead's fiscal stability, lays a foundation for future generations to build, free from the burden of debt or uncertainty.

Documenting the Home's Story

Memorializing the saga of your barndominium, from its inception through every transformation and moment of life within its embrace, adds a rich layer to the legacy you pass on. This documentation, whether in journals, photo albums, or digital archives, is a testament to the love and labor poured into creating a homestead. It offers those who come after a glimpse into the past, a profound and personal connection to the lineage of their home. These chronicles become cherished heirlooms, narratives that bind the generations in a shared story of resilience, creativity, and belonging.

Sustainability and Future-Proofing

The legacy of a barndominium, to endure and remain relevant through generations, must be woven with the principles of sustainability and adaptability. This foresight involves integrating features that reduce the homestead's environmental impact, from renewable energy sources to water conservation and waste reduction systems. But beyond the ecological, future-proofing also means designing with flexibility in mind, creating spaces that can evolve with the changing dynamics of family life and technology. It's a commitment to a home that not only stands the test of time but also remains a beacon of innovation and stewardship, a model for living that harmonizes with the earth and anticipates the future.

In portraying the barndominium as a legacy, planning, documentation, sustainability, and adaptability weave together to form a rich narrative imbued with history, values, and care. It is a testament to a fulfilling life and an invaluable legacy to future generations. By laying the groundwork for this transition, by embedding in every beam and pane the essence of our hopes and dreams, we ensure that the barndominium stands not just as a structure but as a legacy, a homestead that nurtures and inspires generations yet to come.

In reflection, the journey of transforming a barndominium into a lasting legacy encompasses far more than the physical construction or renovation of a dwelling. It involves thoughtful consideration of how the structure interacts with its environment, serves the needs of those who call it home, and how it can continue for generations. Through careful planning, documentation, and a commitment to sustainability, we lay the foundations for a future where our barndominiums stand as monuments to our values, creativity, and love for the land and each other. As we move forward, we carry with us the understanding that our actions today shape the legacy we leave tomorrow, guiding us as we continue to explore the depths of barndominium living and all the possibilities it holds.

CONCLUSION

As we wrap up this journey together, I can't help but reflect on the incredible path we've ventured down—from the seed of creating a barndominium to the blossoming reality of living in one. We've navigated the intricacies of envisioning your dream space, detailed planning, financial foresight, and the creative process of designing and constructing. Together, we've seen how a blend of rustic allure and modern efficiency coexists and thrives in the unique lifestyle a barndominium offers.

The heart of this book was to underscore that barndominium living is within reach for everyone, regardless of budget size. We've explored the avenues of sustainable building, the richness of community life, personal well-being, and the profound satisfaction of crafting a legacy within the walls of a home that truly reflects who you are. With diligent planning, a mindful budget, and a commitment to green practices, the complexities of creating your dream barndominium can be navigated confidently.

Innovation and creativity have been our constant companions on this journey. They've shown us how the marriage of traditional charm with contemporary conveniences doesn't just result in a functional and beautiful dwelling but carves out a deeply personal space and a true reflection of your values and lifestyle.

This book was intended to be your compass and companion, offering guidance from financial insights and design inspirations to hands-on DIY advice and lifestyle considerations. I aimed to make the dream of barndominium living attainable for anyone who dared to dream it.

Now, I encourage you to take that leap. Let the pages of this book guide you as you start sketching out your plans, picking out your tools, and imagining the life that awaits within the barndominium you will create. Embrace every challenge, celebrate every victory, and immerse yourself fully in bringing your dream home to life.

I invite you to share your story with the world. Let your journey inspire others by connecting with fellow barndominium enthusiasts, whether that's through social media, online forums, or local gatherings. There's a whole community out there eager to support you and be part of your adventure.

Thank you, indeed, for walking this path with me. Every step you take toward your barndominium is a step closer to realizing a dream that is uniquely yours. Approach each phase with patience, perseverance, and an unwavering excitement for what's to come. I promise the destination will be worth every moment of the journey.

Warmest wishes and happy building,

M.R. Boss

KEEPING THE DREAM ALIVE

Now that you've equipped yourself with all the tools and insights necessary to turn your barndominium dreams into reality, it's time to pay it forward and share your newfound knowledge with others.

By simply sharing your honest opinion of *Barndominiums: Maximize Design Efficiency for Open-Concept Living* on Amazon, you're not only helping potential readers discover the wealth of information within these pages but also igniting their passion for barndominium living.

Thank you for your invaluable contribution. The spirit of barndominiums thrives when we pass on our knowledge and enthusiasm to others, and you're playing a vital role in keeping that spirit alive.

Your support means the world to us as we continue to inspire and empower dreamers around the globe.

Warm regards,

M.R. BOSS

ADDITIONAL RESOURCES

https://www.BarndominiumLife.com—A comprehensive guide to everything barndominium.

https://www.GreenBuildingAdvisor.com—For sustainable construction tips and eco-friendly materials.

https://www.meetup.com/—Find or start a local barndominium community group near you.

https://buildmax.com/—Dive into the thrill of crafting your dream space while we navigate the challenges for you.

https://jsenterprise1.com/barndominium-landscaping/—Transforming Your Barndominium's Outdoor Space.

RESOURCES

1845 Barndominiums. "1845 Barndominiums." Accessed May 23, 2024. https://www.1845barndominiums.com.

Anderson Jones. "Resolving Construction Disputes: Three Strategies for Issue Resolution," November 30, 2023. https://www.andersonandjones.com/resolving-construction-disputes-three-strategies-for-issue-resolution/.

Anika's DIY Life. "How Barndominium Homes Combine Traditional Rustic Charm With Modern Luxury." Accessed May 23, 2024. https://www.anikasdiylife.com.

Architectural Designs. "Barndominium House Plans," n.d. https://www.architecturaldesigns.com/house-plans/styles/barndominium.

Barndominium Design. "Navigating Barndominium Permits and Codes," n.d. https://barndominium.design/permits.

Cochran, Brice. "The Comprehensive Guide to Barndominiums: A New Trend in Housing." Timber Frame HQ, September 24, 2023. https://timberframehq.com/guide-to-barndominiums/.

Construct Elements. "Average Cost to Build a Barndominium - Detail Guide." Accessed May 23, 2024. https://www.constructelements.com.

Davis, Jon. "Cost Overrun in Construction Projects: Top Strategies to Stay on Budget." Capsule CRM, November 1, 2023. https://capsulecrm.com/blog/const-overrun-construction-projects/.

Foyr. "Color Theory Basics: How To Use Color Theory For Interior Design?," September 13, 2021. https://foyr.com/learn/color-theory-in-interior-design/.

Goldsborough Company. "RainWater Harvesting," n.d. https://www.goldsboroughco.com/for-my-home/rainwater-harvesting.html.

Greenfield, Matt. "Barndominium Cost vs House: Detailed Cost Comparison Guide." Today's Homeowner, August 10, 2021. https://todayshomeowner.com/blog/guides/barndominium-cost-vs-house/.

Hisaka, Mizuki. "How Much Does a Barndominium Cost? [2024 Cost]." Angi, January 3, 2024. https://www.angi.com/articles/barndominium-cost.htm

Kathy Kuo Home. "6 Design Tips for an Open Floor Plan Home Design," February 7, 2017. https://www.kathykuohome.com/blog/6-design-tips-for-an-open-floor-plan/.

Liggett, Billy. "Modern & Rustic: Family Introduces the 'Barndominium' to Sanford." THE RANT, January 31, 2024. https://rantnc.com/2024/01/31/modern-rustic-family-introduces-the-barndominium-to-sanford/.

Metal Building Homes. "The Ultimate Barndominium Guide (Info, Plans & Pricing In 2024)." Accessed May 23, 2024. https://www.metal-building-homes.com.

Mmminimal. "Barndominium Life: Farmhouse Living," July 17, 2023. https://mmminimal.com/barndominium-life-wrangle-farmhouse-living-with-this-trending-home/.

O'Connor, Michael. "6 Expert Tips For Choosing a Barndominium Builder," February 17, 2022. https://www.barndominiumlife.com/choosing-a-barndominium-builder/.

Rainplanner. "Catch the Rain: Rainwater Harvesting Systems." Rainplan, April 6, 2022. https://myrainplan.com/rainwater-harvesting-systems/.

Redfin. "What is a Barndominium? Everything You Need to Know." Accessed May 23, 2024. https://www.redfin.com.

Roper Buildings. "Barndominiums." Accessed May 23, 2024. https://www.roperbuildings.com.

Scott, Aaron. "Potential Issues for First Time Barndominium Builders." BuildMax, October 28, 2021. https://buildmax.com/potential-issues-for-first-time-barndominium-builders/.

"Tackling Common Barndominium Construction Challenges." BuildMax, October 20, 2023. https://buildmax.com/tackling-common-barndominium-construction-challenges/.

Tampasis, Jennifer. "Smart Home Integration: Tech Solutions for Modern Living." Jennifer Lynn Interiors, March 1, 2024. https://jenniferlynninteriors.com/2024/03/01/smart-home-integration/.

Texas Country Charmers. "Barndominium House Plans in Texas." Accessed May 23, 2024. https://www.texascountrycharmers.com.

The Barndominium Company. "Barndominium Floor Plans | Stock & Custom," n.d. https://thebarndominiumcompany.com/floor-plans/.

Travel Tweaks. "Embracing Rustic Charm and Modern Living With Barndominiums." May 23, 2024. https://www.traveltweaks.com.

Turner, Rachel. "20 Brilliant Multifunctional Furniture Ideas for Small Homes." *A House in the Hills* (blog), June 6, 2023. https://ahouseinthehills.com/brilliant-multifunctional-furniture-ideas-for-small-homes/.

WTW. "Construction Supply Chain Risk Report 2023," July 11, 2023. https://www.wtwco.com/en-us/insights/2023/07/construction-supply-chain-risk-report-2023.

Made in the USA
Coppell, TX
05 December 2024

41729683R00105